Re:CONSIDERING

THE FREEDOM TRAP

Priyan Max Jeganathan

a. Acorn Press

Published by Acorn Press, an imprint of Bible Society Australia, in partnership with the Centre for Public Christianity.

ACN 127 775 973
GPO Box 4161
Sydney NSW 2001
Australia

www.publicchristianity.org

© Centre for Public Christianity, 2025. All rights reserved.

ISBN 978-0-647-53387-1 (pbk)
ISBN 978-0-647-53388-8 (ebk)

A catalogue record for this book is available from the National Library of Australia

Apart from any fair dealing for the purposes of private study, research, criticism or review, no part of this work may be reproduced by electronic or other means without the permission of the publisher.

Priyan Max Jeganathan asserts his right under section 193 of the *Copyright Act 1968* (Cth) to be identified as the author of this work.

Scripture quotations are taken from the Holy Bible, New International Version® Anglicized, NIV® Copyright © 1979, 1984, 2011 by Biblica Inc.® Used by permission. All rights reserved worldwide.

Editor: Lauren Switzer

Cover and text design: John Healy

About the Centre for Public Christianity

What is the good life?
What does it mean to be human?
Where can I find meaning?
Who can I trust?

In sceptical and polarised times, the Centre for Public Christianity (CPX) seeks to engage the public with a clear, balanced, and surprising picture of the Christian faith. A not-for-profit media company, since 2007 CPX has been joining the dots between contemporary culture and the enduring story of Jesus in the articles, podcasts, books, documentaries, and other resources we produce.

We believe Christianity still has something vital to say about life's biggest questions. Find out more about our team and the work we do at www.publicchristianity.org or follow us on Facebook, X and Instagram.

About the author

Priyan (Max) Jeganathan is a Senior Research Fellow at the Centre for Public Christianity (CPX) and an Associate Speaker at The Oxford Centre for Christian Apologetics (OCCA). A former lawyer and political and policy adviser, Max was educated at the Australian National University and the University of Oxford and is undertaking a PhD in Law. He has spoken in universities, political institutions and businesses, including Samsung, Lego, Goldman Sachs and Amazon. Max's writing has appeared in *The Sydney Morning Herald*, *The Age*, *The Canberra Times*, *The Guardian* and the ABC's *Religion and Ethics Report*. His hobbies are fried chicken, and making his wife and kids laugh.

CONTENTS

1. THE LONGING FOR FREEDOM 1

2. OLD FREEDOM. .9

3. NEW FREEDOM 15

4. THE TRAP. 21
   Trapped by choice .23
   Trapped by consequences 27
   Trapped by success. 32
   Trapped by technology 45

5. ESCAPING THE FREEDOM TRAP 55
   The challenge of autonomy 56
   Re-imagining the 'good life'. 64

6. RECLAIMING FREEDOM 75
   Purpose-driven freedom 75
   What's love got to do with it? 84
   Reclaiming freedom in everyday life. 90
      i. Slowing down and paying attention 94
      ii. Limiting choice where we can 97
      iii. Being kind .100
      iv. Investing in relationships. 103
   Conclusion 106

For Appa and Amma, who showed me that Freedom begins with faith, and for Fiona, Zachary, Arielle and Grace, who showed me that Freedom is about other people.

Re:CONSIDERING

1. THE LONGING FOR FREEDOM

An old man in a white suit stood up from behind his small market stall on the outskirts of Tehran. In the tropical humidity, he smiled as his ice-white hair and matching goatee cut through the monotony of another scorching day in the marketplace. The weather was hot. The usual buzz of buyers and sellers formed its familiar soundtrack of haggling. Nothing to see here. But then, something unusual happened. He began to dance. He swayed. He grooved. And after a few minutes, people started noticing. Then, they started gathering around him. He serenaded a growing crowd that was drawn to him with every movement, every song and every beat. A group of young men joined in, chanting songs back at the 70-year-old Pied Piper. Multiple smartphones captured the moment, and within minutes, it went viral. The man's name was Sadegh Bana Motejaded. Fittingly and wonderfully, his nickname was Booghy. You can't make this stuff up. The moment sparked a week-long viral trend across Iran of people posting videos on social media of themselves dancing. People were dancing in the streets, in sporting arenas, in schools, in shopping centres, in cafes and restaurants … everywhere.

Amusing? Sure. But no big deal. Surely similarly amusing yet short-lived and inconsequential social media fads come and go every week. The reason this one was more interesting is because dancing in public is illegal in Iran. It was a statement, a declaration, a movement – a glimpse of freedom. The existential human resistance to subjugation was given physical expression through something as simple and primal as dancing. To mashup Booghy's viral dancing with an old battle cry for freedom: They can take our lives, but they can never take our ability to dance! One Iranian DJ said that, 'it's a way of protesting and demanding our freedom and happiness.'[1]

The linking of freedom with happiness is not new. It underpins the Magna Carta, the historic document that declared that kings and governments are not above the law. The Magna Carta was one of the original birth certificates

---

[1] Farnaz Fassihi, 'A viral dance and happiness campaign frustrates Iran's clerics', *The New York Times*, 17 December 2023, accessed 15 June 2024. https://www.nytimes.com/2023/12/16/world/middleeast/a-viral-dance-and-happiness-campaign-frustrates-irans-clerics.html

1. The Longing for Freedom

of modern democracy, and freedom was central to its foundation. But the human longing for freedom is not just political in its expression. It's also personal, offering up glimpses of itself in our movies, music, literature and mythology.

In his 1958 classic children's story 'Yertle the Turtle', Dr Seuss writes of a colony of turtles ruled belligerently by their self-proclaimed king, Yertle. Yertle exploits and oppresses his fellow turtles, much to the dismay of many in the colony. However, thanks to a little turtle named Mac, Yertle's autocratic rule was not to last. Channelling Booghy from Tehran and the Magna Carta, Mac quietly launched a revolution that brought an end to Yertle's rule. The final line of the story gloriously reads:

> *And today the great Yertle that Marvellous he,*
> *Is King of the Mud. That is all he can see.*
> *And the turtles, of course … all the turtles are free*
> *As turtles and, maybe, all creatures should be.*[2]

Children's stories. The fall of the Berlin Wall. The constitutional revolutions that birthed modern democracy. The viral dance sensation sparked by a fish market owner. They all have something in common. They all give expression to the human appetite for freedom.

---

[2] Dr. Seuss, *Yertle the turtle and other stories,* HarperCollins USA, 1986.

In the middle of the Cold War, some of the USSR's biggest challenges included trying to get its young people to stop wearing American jeans and listening to Western music. For these young people, freedom was a more important impulse than patriotism. And on some level, at least, it seems like a healthy impulse. According to the world's leading economists, no country with a truly free media has ever experienced a famine since the Industrial Revolution.[3] Getting people to not seek freedom is like getting a five-year-old not to seek ice cream. Not gonna happen.

At the start of America's War of Independence, the Americans (then a disparate scattering of British colonies) were the freest and most lightly taxed people in the world. But it wasn't enough and they started a war over liberty anyway. It was the principle. They wanted to govern themselves. Politically and economically, they had it made, but their revolution wasn't political or economic – it was, at its most basic level, anthropological. It wasn't merely about what they wanted to do. It was also about what they wanted to be. Free. As the philosopher Hegel put it, 'The history of the world is none other than the progress of the consciousness of freedom.'[4]

---

[3] Amartya Sen. *Development as freedom*, Alfred A Knopf, New York, 1999, p 16.
[4] GWF Hegel, *The Philosophy of history* (J Sibree trans.),

1. The Longing for Freedom

From the kid who can't fight the urge to touch that exhibit at the museum because they've been told not to touch it, to the reluctant adult who struggles to stop completely at a stop sign before driving on – there's something very human about 'raging against the machine'. The instincts we have to fight off constraints continue to underpin both the stability and instability of our world. As I write this, two wars are being fought in the name of freedom – one in Ukraine and another in the Middle East, with all sides using claims to freedom to make their case. Many powerful nations from the East and West continue to flex the muscles of their navies, missile systems, economies and exercise soft power – often in the name of their freedom to do so. Protests, anger and bitterness continue to pervade various political movements – both conservative and progressive – with both sides regularly citing 'freedom' as the ideal for which they're fighting.

Freedom – somehow – goes to the heart of what it means to be human. We've built our nations on it. We've built our lives on it. We've built our happiness on it – the idea that people can and should be free. Free from slavery. Free from poverty. Free from oppression. Free from discrimination.

Dover Publications, New York, 1956 [1837], p 33.

But modern times have infused old notions of freedom with new meaning. Freedom has been valorised, embellished and accessorised. Voting rights aren't enough. Property rights aren't enough. Civil rights aren't enough. We want sexual freedom, financial freedom and emotional freedom too. We want faster phones, greener cars, smarter appliances and unlimited live streaming. Our drive to be free from oppression remains. But our modern notions of freedom come wrapped in desire, distraction and entertainment. Modernity has put everything from movies to music to shopping to pornography at our fingertips.

We now demand to be free from inconvenience, free from offence and free from limits – free from anything that stands in the way of what we want. No song better sums up the modern understanding of freedom than Frank Sinatra's 1969 hit 'My Way'. It continues to feature on our airwaves more than 50 years after its first release.

The entrenchment of the internet and smart-phone as pillars of modern life, and the digitalisation of everything from friendship to shopping both demand a closer look at what freedom is. Any foray into such vast waters will be necessarily limited. This short book seeks to make a small contribution to the broader conversation that is needed around how we moderns feel about,

1. The Longing for Freedom

think about – or fail to think about – what freedom is. We are healthier, wealthier and freer than ever before, but our measures of life satisfaction don't seem to be increasing at the same pace as the speed of our computers.[5]

St Paul – one of Christianity's early pioneers – wrote in an ancient letter to the Galatian church, 'You, my brothers and sisters, were called to be free.'[6] It's a shame he didn't include a footnote explaining what he meant by 'free'. It's something we need to think about more carefully. Let's do that.

---

[5] Sherry Tuckle, *Alone together: why we expect more from technology and less from each other*, Basic Books, New York, 2011, pp 378–421.
[6] Galatians 5:13.

Re:CONSIDERING

2. OLD FREEDOM

In his book on political communication, *Don't Think of an Elephant*,[1] political scientist George Lakoff notes the use of Orwellian language by dictatorial and totalitarian regimes. If democracy is so bad, it's curious that its staunchest critics continue to pay lip service to it. The government of China proclaims the democratic nature of the operations of the Chinese Communist Party. The government of Iran calls itself a republic. And perhaps most amusingly, the totalitarian government of North Korea insists that its nation be called the Democratic People's Republic of Korea. This suggests that even autocrats understand that freedom at its most fundamental level is something that is viewed positively by people across cultures, even when their governments do little to honour it.

As is the case with most modern notions, the idea of 'freedom' has ancient beginnings. There have been uprisings in the ancient world that

---

[1] George Lakoff, *Don't think of an elephant!: know your values and frame the debate*, Chelsea Green Publishing Company, White River Junction VT, 2004.

give us glimpses of the intrinsic human longing for freedom. Slave and oppressed worker revolts in ancient Rome and ancient Egypt suggest that collective human oppression has rarely been met with passive acceptance for long.

However, our modern liberal understanding of individual freedom seems to be traceable to a series of events and systems of thinking that began bubbling up around 1,000 years ago. The Magna Carta established the principle that governments were not above the law. Such thinking gave rise to what we now know as modern parliaments. The Middle Ages also gave rise to the idea of common law – the idea that there should be fairness and consistency in how people understand their freedoms and make sense of what's allowed and not allowed, enabling society to cohesively function. It all seemed to be about protecting people from their governments and ensuring that governments did not have unlimited power. And while it hasn't been perfect, it hasn't been an abject failure either. This democratic experiment hasn't really reduced the level of grumpiness that we have with our leaders, but on some level, they are held to account, at least in societies with genuine elections and a free media.

While many strands of thinking contributed to the story of freedom – from the ancient civilisations of Greece, Rome and Egypt to the world wars of the 20th century – underlying much of the story has been a distinctly Judeo-Christian notion of the individual. The ubiquity of the Christian idea of the individual was a gradual phenomenon, making its way from the early Christian scriptures through medieval Christendom and 12th-century canon law[2] through the various European Enlightenments and, eventually, into modern political and legal parlance and of course, the lyrics of Frank Sinatra. Now, we're all encouraged to do life 'my way'. As historian Tom Holland observes in relation to the idea of human rights, 'The West, over the duration of its global hegemony, had become skilled in the art of repackaging Christian concepts for non-Christian audiences.'[3]

The ideals of freedom of speech, thought, conscience and association have formed the moral platform on which modern Western society has been built, for better or worse. As a result, fidelity to freedom is a mark of the modern enlightened mind. Discrimination, exclusion, oppression and bigotry are all – understandably – deemed opposed to freedom and, therefore, rendered evils

---

[2] Nicholas Wolterstorff, *Justice: rights and wrongs*, Princeton University Press, Princeton, 2008, ch 2.
[3] Tom Holland, *Dominion: the making of the Western mind*, Little, Brown and Company, New York, 2019, p 57.

that should be eradicated. At first glance, this seems to be a good thing. However, within these assumptions lies the possibility that when freedom is embellished, its distortions are not properly interrogated, leaving modern society exposed, not to an erosion of freedom, but to anything and everything that uses freedom as a bodyguard to smuggle its way into our schools, workplaces and news cycles.

Ancient and medieval times offered glimpses of the different frames of thinking that mark the distinctions between traditional understandings of freedom and modern understandings of freedom. The word 'freedom' is taken from two words. The first is the Latin word *libertus*, which refers to rights. The second is the German word *vridom*, which refers to freedom from enslavement. Today, both definitions of freedom continue to be relevant, but the former has taken centre stage, and that has made all the difference.

At the level of political systems, constitutions and human rights, the march of freedom has been – on any measure – a good thing. However, the project of making sure governments can't do whatever they want has now been accessorised with a newly embellished conception of freedom. That is, the idea that we should be allowed to do whatever we want, whenever we want, however we

2. Old Freedom

want. The big-picture ideal of freedom has been adorned by a more personal, practical brand of individual freedom that fits in our smartphones. Freedom has been reconceived and recalibrated – morphing from a political objective that underpins our societies to a psychological need that is designed to enable us to realise our desires. With our digital wallets, online shopping baskets and smartphones in tow, we have happily migrated from the idea of 'freedom from governments' to 'freedom for me'. While ancient understandings centred mainly on how people related to their governments, more recent times have seen freedom being understood personally rather than collectively. We've shifted from seeking to build cohesive societies to furthering individual rights. Not necessarily a bad thing. But the fleas come with the dog.

Some of these embellishments began long before the information technology, contactless payments and personal computing revolutions of the 1990s and 2000s. Medieval movements like the 'Brotherhood of the Free Spirit' took the idea of personal freedom to mean a total denial of all restraints and limitations, including those of morality. Looking back, these hyper-liberal ideas seem like early whispers of what later thinkers like Frederick Nietzsche and Ayn Rand picked up on.

The philosophical mould had been cast. It was just a matter of a few rounds of industrial revolutions, the internet, modern marketing and consumer culture, before self-focused ideas of freedom could take full flight.

Re:CONSIDERING

3. NEW FREEDOM

We often think of liberalism as an imperfect but simple enough political idea that centres on the principle that people should be free. But – like any system of thought – there's a little more to it. The last thousand years or so have not merely given rise to 'liberalism', as such, but to a family of liberalisms, each with subtle but significant differences in their understanding of freedom. This is not a book about political science, but – as is the case with any journey – it's worth taking a moment to work out how we got here.

The modern idea of freedom is based on two varieties of liberalism. The first is the idea that when people are given freedom, they will ultimately agree on what a good and flourishing society looks like. The second is the idea that people should be able to do whatever they want, provided it doesn't hurt other people. Modern societies tend to toggle between these two systems of thinking. But there has been a gradual shift from the former to the latter. The reason the distinction is important and relevant is because the original varieties of liberalism refused to give up on the ancient notion of a 'common good' – held across the board by the ancient Romans, Greeks, Egyptians, Hebrews, pagans and early Christians. Nowadays, there's nothing common about the good. We are each called on to work out what it is for ourselves. You do you. Your best self. Your best life. We can't seem to get Frank Sinatra out of our heads. And no one seems interested in changing the playlist.

Maybe modern liberal societies have just had their hands full over the last thousand years or so. Maybe we've been too busy to rethink what freedom is and what it means to us – what with all of our leaps forward in technology, finance, education and entertainment, coupled with threats to our way of life. Repeatedly having to defend freedom against fascism, communism, socialism, totalitarianism and a handful of other menacing 'isms' is tiring work. It seems that we haven't spent as much time and energy considering what freedom consists of as we have defending and protecting it. Instead, most of us have settled into cruise control, comfortable with our assumption that everything will work out fine if limits are minimised. The more that people can choose for themselves, the better.

3. New Freedom

A few industrial revolutions and a couple of hundred years later, our freedom-fuelled recipe for this 'modern happiness project' is rarely questioned. But it's still based on the cocktail of ancient traditions that we have embellished into our modern idea of individual freedom. As far as ideas go, it has many grandparents – from the ancient Greeks to the ancient Hebrews to the early Christians to the modern revolutionaries of the North Atlantic. Like any grandchild, modern freedom reflects glimpses of its ancestors, but it also has its own mind and continues to insist on its independence.

Before America's Declaration of Independence, freedom was about life, liberty and property. It was primarily political, civil and economic. Significantly, Thomas Jefferson swapped out 'property' for 'happiness'. It might seem like a minor 'tracked change' in the Word document of history, but it highlighted a shift in thinking that forms the backdrop of modern life – the idea that life is about making ourselves happy with the fewest constraints and limits possible.

Understanding modern freedom is synonymous with understanding the emergence of the modern self as it has embraced modern technology. A cavalcade of books, articles and conferences have sought to unpack what modern personhood looks like. I'm not trying to add to that scholarship here. However – to summarise, one conclusion has been that modern identity is increasingly unencumbered by ancient notions of human nature, constraints or tradition. As put by the wonderfully blunt political theorist John Gray, the idea of hyper-liberal freedom is about enabling people to entirely define their own identities – 'the end point of individualism.'[1] Interestingly, Gray goes on to assert that, in his view, living like this can be nothing more than a private fantasy.

Those of us who live by the creed of 'expressive individualism' – the idea that self-expression and self-fulfilment reign supreme – are living out the latest version of freedom on the shoulders of technologists. The telegraph, telephone and internet boosted our freedom to communicate. The electric light gave us the freedom to extend our days into the night. Antibiotics gave us freedom from countless diseases and – at least temporarily – from death. But our personal empowerment has not been linear. It has been exponentially exponential – increasing at an increasing rate. The acceleration in technological advances continues at a frenzied pace that is difficult to measure. It took around 2.4 million years for our ancestors

---

[1] John Gray, *The new leviathans: thoughts after liberalism*, Allen Lane, London, 2023, p 109.

3. New Freedom

to control fire and use it for cooking, but only 66 years between the Wright brothers' first flight and humankind's first steps on the moon.[2]

We're getting really good at getting really good at what we do. With every advance, personal freedom – on some level – is growing. As ever, humankind is on the prowl for new heights to scale, new ceilings to crash through and new frontiers to explore. To the old pillars of success – achievement and accumulation – we have added status, convenience and pleasurable experiences. Almost every technological advance is viewed through these newly defined lenses of happiness.

Advances in digital technology have unleashed human capability, capacity and functionality. The onset of generative artificial intelligence, the universalising of information access, and the boosting of data processing, transmission speeds and global interconnectedness mean that we can access more information and entertainment more quickly than ever. Our computers are getting faster, our cars are getting greener and our appliances are getting smarter. Our global net worth has tripled since 2000.[3] As a result, we are told that we are

---

[2] Max Roser, *Technology over the long run*, Our World in Data, February 2023, accessed July 2024. https://ourworldindata.org/technology-long-run

[3] Lola Woetzel, Jan Mischke, Any Madgavkar, Eckart Windhagen, Sven Smit, Michael Birshan, Szabolcs Kemeny

freer than ever to do whatever we want, whenever we want, however we want. We are – it seems – closer than ever to limitlessness.

What could possibly go wrong?

---

and Rebecca J. Anderson, *The rise and rise of the global balance sheet: how productively are we using our wealth*, Mckinsey Global Institute website, November 2021, accessed August 2024. https://www.mckinsey.com/industries/financial-services/our-insights/the-rise-and-rise-of-the-global-balance-sheet-how-productively-are-we-using-our-wealth

Re:CONSIDERING

4. THE TRAP

Leo Tolstoy's short story *How Much Land Does a Man Need?*[1] tells of a Russian peasant named Pakhom. Demonstrating a number of characteristics of the modern self, Pakhom longs for quick wealth and fast success. To satisfy his desire to be free of all fear and constraints, he approaches a group of wealthy landowners – the Bashkirs – to negotiate a large block of land on favourable terms. The chief of the Bashkirs offers Pakhom a deal. He may choose any point on their land and begin there at sunrise the following day. From the moment he sets off, he has the full day of sunlight to traverse as large a perimeter as he is able to on foot. Whatever perimeter he secures is his for a nominal sum. However, he must return to his starting point before the sun sets. If not, the Bashkirs keep Pakhom's money, and he gets nothing. The next day at sunrise, Pakhom sets off to secure his fortune, excited about the vast tracts

---

[1] Leo Tolstoy, *How much land does a man need?*, Penguin Classics, London, 2024.

of land that could be his by sunset. As the sun begins to set, however, he still has a way to go to return to his starting point. Exerting himself to the point of exhaustion, Pakhom sprints for the finish line, with fascinated crowds looking on. Moments before the sun drops behind the horizon, he reaches his goal. However, the drain and strain on his body has been too great. He'd acquired what he wanted but misread himself. Before the reader has a chance to celebrate with Tolstoy's protagonist, Pakhom promptly drops dead before he can take hold of his prize. The final scene of the story is of Pakhom's body being buried in a regular-sized grave – thereby answering the question: How much land does a man need?

The story reads as tragedy and comedy. But beneath its unsatisfying narrative arc lies a lesson that gives us pause for thought. Striving for what we want is not always a bad thing. But it always comes with a price. As an old Spanish proverb puts it: 'Take what you want, said God. Take it and pay for it.' All exercises of freedom come with a context, a cost and consequences.

Perhaps we think we are living with blank cheques rather than maxed-out credit cards. Have we been so enamoured with the benefits of limitlessness that we've been wilfully ignoring the fine print? Or worse, have we been so subtly lulled into obliviousness that we are blind to freedom's nature, costs and consequences? Are we in a freedom trap?

Trapped by choice

In her book *The Art of Choosing*, social psychologist Sheena Iyengar explores the surprising and fascinating aspects of decision-making. Iyengar agrees with the notion that we are a little obsessed with freedom. In her words, we have a 'knee-jerk negative response' to anything that might have control over us, and that is a result of putting 'choice on a pedestal, so much so that we expect to be able to bend everything to our will'.[2]

According to the research, choice is not a bad thing in and of itself. However, there's fine print that we tend to ignore. One study sums up the case for being a bit more careful and thoughtful about our valorisation of choice – and it all begins with a jar of jam. Experimenters studied the decision-making, feelings and choices of different shoppers who were hunting for jam in a supermarket, while changing the jam varieties available from time to time.

---

[2] Sheena Iyengar, *Art of choosing*, Hachette Book Group, New York, 2010, p 175.

The results showed that the fewer the number of jam flavours people were given to choose from, the more likely they were to buy a jar of jam.[3] The more jam options there were, the more confused and anxious people became. And even if they did end up buying jam, they took longer to do so. Obviously, buying jam is a little more trivial than choosing a life partner, voting in an election, or being able to read, speak and think freely. But the principle is clear: when it comes to choice, more is not always better. 'More choice leads to less satisfaction or fulfilment or happiness.'[4]

I get it. Staying with the theme of generously sugared products, I continue to be simultaneously overwhelmed and unimpressed with the seemingly unstoppable proliferation of Tim Tam™ varieties on offer. In a perpetual exhibition of product adaptation for innovation's sake, Arnott's (the company that manufactures Tim Tam biscuits) has crossbred Tim Tams – originally a double-layered milk-chocolate biscuit – with coconuts, piña coladas, espresso martinis, peanut butter and even paprika. Preparing for a 'Tim Tam Slam'[5]

---

[3] Ibid., ch 6.

[4] Ibid., pp 178–179.

[5] I hesitate to assume that this requires a footnote. However, in the interests of thoroughness: a Tim Tam Slam refers to the age-old Australian cultural tradition of taking two very small bites from diagonally opposing corners of a Tim Tam

has become a much more confusing and complicated process.

I know some would disagree. Perhaps unsurprisingly, the jam-choosing study and its findings have been angrily labelled by some as 'anti-freedom'. Somehow, the tyranny of only having six or seven types of jam to choose from is unacceptable to some of our freedom-loving modern consumer sentiments. If anything, such reactions affirm the point: maybe we're a little overprotective when it comes to thinking about choice. Like Gollum and the 'One Ring', it's become our *precious*. It might not be time for a trip to Mordor, but perhaps it's time to rethink the unquestioned virtue of unlimited choice.

Author and journalist Malcolm Gladwell writes of another study akin to the jam-choosing experiment – just a few aisles over in the pasta section of the supermarket. In research conducted on spaghetti sauce for the food company Prego,[6] it was found that while there was no single perfect spaghetti sauce that would please everyone,

---

chocolate biscuit, and then effectively using the remaining Tim Tam as a straw, by sipping milk, coffee or tea through it. Following the sip, you are left with a deliciously soaked milk-infused Tim Tam, to be shoved ('slammed') in your mouth and enjoyed.

[6] Malcolm Gladwell, *What the dog saw and other adventures*, Penguin Press, New York, 2009, pp 64–91, ebook.

consumer preferences came down to three main categories of spaghetti sauce – plain, spicy and extra chunky. Yes, people have different preferences, and in our modern age of invention and consumerism, you would expect that consumer demand will increase the range of what's for sale. However, when it comes to the human pursuit of happiness, a never-ending plethora of options doesn't seem particularly helpful.

From time to time, my wife and I find ourselves with a few spare moments to watch something on the TV. However, between the line-up of apps and live streaming options available, the breadth of choice often overwhelms. All too often, we end up watching previews and trailers or switching out of something after starting it. Before we know it, our time is up. We could have watched anything, but we had to choose something, and we didn't. The possibilities seemed endless, but we turned it into a trap.

Former US president Barack Obama famously only owned suits in two colours – dark grey and dark blue – which he alternated throughout his presidency. His reason for this was simple. Obama recognised that on any given day, he had a limited amount of decision-making energy. Using even a small amount up on trivial things like what he was going to wear was a waste of his time and his headspace. From the then leader of the free world, it's a telling reminder. Anyone who's planned a wedding, built a house or selected a paint colour for a home renovation will understand. It's nice to be able to choose. But it always takes time, and it's not always easy. The more options we have, the more likely we are to second-guess ourselves, the more we might put pressure on ourselves and the more exhausted we become. Choice has the capacity to paralyse, exhaust and frustrate at least as much as a lack of choice does. Whether you're the president of the United States or just a punter choosing jam, pasta sauce, Tim Tams or what to watch on TV, the first principles are clear. Choice is good, but more is not always better. Limitless choices have their limits.

Trapped by consequences

The 2011 sci-fi thriller *Limitless* – starring Bradley Cooper – follows the story of struggling writer Eddie Morra, who discovers a newly invented nootropic pill engineered to heighten the abilities, capacities and performance of anyone who takes it. Armed with super senses, super strength and super intelligence, Eddie clicks into high gear. His personal and professional life explodes with wealth and power, going beyond his wildest dreams. He is, for all intents and purposes, a man living without limits. However, that isn't the end of the story. Unsavoury characters discover the secret to Eddie's success and come after him. He's forced to go to great lengths to protect himself and to hide his stash of the new wonder drug, which, of course, he has become fully dependent on. The film ends (spoiler alert) with a perilous escape from his pursuers and a realisation that his newfound limitlessness wasn't worth it. The final scene of the film is a flashforward to a newly enlightened Eddie Morra – running as a candidate for the US Senate – who has trained his senses naturally to achieve impressive and superior performance within the natural limits of humankind. More human. More measured. More thoughtful. Less limitless. And, importantly, more focused on a particular outcome than on the unflinching pursuit of limitlessness for its own sake.

The film is a reminder of three things that we often ignore in the midst of our freedom-soaked aspirations.

4. The Trap

   i. Freedom offers choices.
   ii. Choices have consequences.
   iii. Consequences constrain.

We might be able to choose from 40 different types of toothbrushes, but we don't get to choose whether or not we brush our teeth. Well, perhaps we do. But a failure to brush our teeth will lead to an array of other, more costly choices – between dentists, orthodontists and periodontists. The economic principle of opportunity cost refers to the price we pay for doing something, given what else we could have done had we not done that thing. The opportunity cost of watching something on Netflix for a couple of hours is effectively anything else that I could have spent two hours on – reading, cooking, having a drink with my wife or walking the dog. There's not necessarily a right or wrong with these examples. The point is that my time can only be spent one way. And however I chose to spend it, there were other things that I implicitly chose not to do. All choices have consequences and opportunity costs – things that they lead to and things we could have done instead.

Books, life hacks, courses and seminars abound on how to manage our time and become more productive. What these do – the good ones anyway – is help us to more thoughtfully arrange our life to account for opportunity cost. They're an implicit recognition of the fact that every time we use our freedom, it costs us something. Every use of freedom gives some of it away.

As I've explained, our choices have consequences that constrain us. But there's another way in which the consequences of our choices affect us. It's when our choices – and freedoms – rub up against the freedoms of others. This pretty much accounts for every conflict in human history. From world wars to skirmishes in kindergarten playgrounds, conflict at its core is usually an expression of opposing declarations of freedom. One country's freedom to assert sovereignty over its territory frequently rubs up against the freedom of minority groups in that country to govern themselves. My freedom to drive my car really fast can easily conflict with your freedom to cross the road safely. My desire to be free from racial discrimination can rub up against your freedom of speech. Your desire to be free from poverty can rub up against my desire to be free from taxes. My freedom to watch sport after a long day at work can rub up against my children's freedom to watch *Bluey*. (Thankfully, I love *Bluey*, so the last one is easily dealt with, but it's a rare exception.) Cohesive societies, harmonious communities and functioning families demand multiple compromises on different freedoms from all of us.

4. The Trap

Most freedoms that we take for granted are not exercised without limit. I value my freedom of speech, but I relinquish some of it when I choose to sit in a movie theatre and quietly watch a movie without vociferously declaring my opinions of the movie while others are trying to watch it. By attending my local church regularly, I exercise the freedom of religion and association. But for others to enjoy those same freedoms, my freedom of association needs to restrict my ability to form an organisation to incite violence or hatred against other religious groups.

Of course, we all draw the line at different places, but we all draw lines. We have to. Because freedom isn't one thing, and it isn't just mine. The only time you find freedom in the singular form is in the dictionary. Everywhere else, it's about balancing differing and often competing freedoms.

The consequences of our choices point to the reality that our freedoms play out in the daily compromises of real life, where rival political opinions, religious faiths and supporters of warring football teams must somehow coexist. We all live in an interconnected web of choices, consequences and constraints. Every exercise of our freedoms has to be lived out and put up with by our future selves and by those around us. Through our technology, engineering and imaginations, we can keep on shedding limits, but we can never escape the consequences of our growing limitlessness.

Trapped by success

In 1831, a young French politician packed his bags and set sail across the Atlantic. He was on a mission to closely examine the new democratic experiment that was happening in the group of former British colonies now known as the United States of America. His name was Alexis de Tocqueville, and the book he wrote following his travels offered some fascinating insights on freedom, happiness and democracy in America. Like Mac, the turtle – who ended the reign of King Yertle – de Tocqueville was a lover of freedom, declaring his foremost passion as 'the love of liberty and human dignity.'[7] However, his travels across the United States offer interesting reading for anyone trying to make sense of what freedom has to do with success in the 21st century. He saw 19th-century America as the great hope – an

---

[7] Alexis de Tocqueville, *Selected letters on politics and society* (R Boesche ed, J Toupin and R Boesche trans), University of California Press, Berkeley, 1985, p 115.

4. The Trap

embodiment of how freedom, prosperity, virtue and happiness could be brought together. But it wasn't all, as the saying goes, 'beer and skittles'. In one telling comment, de Tocqueville remarked:

> In America I have seen the freest best educated of men in circumstances the happiest to be found in the world; yet it seemed to me that a cloud habitually hung on their brow and they seemed serious and almost sad even in their pleasures.[8]

According to de Tocqueville, the exciting new freedom-fest was accompanied by invisible forces that took some of the shine off of this new 'happiness project'. Even free people, it seems, have a cloud constantly hanging over them. It's a cloud called 'success'.

In his book *The Pearl*,[9] the novelist John Steinbeck tells the story of a pearl diver named Kino, who seeks his fortune diving for pearls in the Gulf of Mexico. One day, he comes across a pearl that is larger than anything he could have imagined. Kino is so certain that his discovery will lead to his and his family's happiness that he commits all of his efforts to protecting it and to turning it into the material wealth that he seeks so badly. However, thieves catch up with him, and

---

[8] Alexis de Tocqueville, *Democracy in America* (JP Mayer ed, G Lawrence trans), Anchor Books, New York, 1969, p 536.
[9] John Steinbeck, *The pearl*, Viking Press, New York, 1947.

in a tragic altercation, he, his wife and the pearl survive, but his young son is tragically killed. The story has chilling echoes of Tolstoy's *How Much Land Does a Man Need?*' and Bradley Cooper's performance in *Limitless*. It unpacks something more invisible yet more influential than the human drive for success – the unquestioned acceptance of what success looks like and the cost of pursuing it without limits. Today, these success markers largely coalesce around wealth, achievement, status and pleasurable experiences. We are told that we can do anything we want and that whatever we choose to do, we should do it our way. However, what we are not told is that no matter what we choose, for it to be considered successful, it has to fit with predetermined modern ideas of success – usually some combination of achievement, accumulation and status – as determined by shifting currents directed by celebrity culture, rich lists, influencers and social expectations. We might get to choose how we get there, but we don't get to entirely define success for ourselves.

Author and lecturer Christopher Watkin makes the point that modern life is such that we're never fully free from constraints. Rather, when we try to trade oppression for freedom, we tend to smuggle in new sources of oppression to replace the old.[10]

---

[10] Christopher Watkin, *Biblical critical theory: how the*

4. The Trap

Peer pressure, social expectations, personal ambition and popularity all quickly step in as our new overlords. How liberating *is* freedom, if we are effectively forced to point it at things out of the bounds of our choices? We can do what we want, but we are railroaded into where we're going. Personal freedom comes with the fine print of a predetermined common horizon of success. We're told that we can do anything and be anything, but the modern example of a successful person doesn't leave much wriggle room. It usually comes down to how much we've achieved, how much we've accumulated, what others think of us and our levels of pleasure and comfort.

When the Apple corporation sought to break into the lucrative and growing market of personal computing, its CEO Steve Jobs chose 'Think different' for its advertising slogan. It was a stirring call to non-conformity that sought to ride the wave of youthful individualism that had been sparked through the sexual revolution, anti-war and hippie movements of the 1960s and '70s. And it worked. Apple established a computing brand that was young, fresh, creative and individualised. In an industry plagued with beige panels and monochrome tones, Apple pumped out designs

Bible's unfolding story makes sense of modern life and culture, Zondervan Academic, Grand Rapids, 2022, p 266.

that were white, bright and fresh. However, as its corporate success and market penetration grew, so did its social prominence. The idea of individuality becomes harder to sell when everyone is conforming to one idea of non-conformity. Flash forward a few decades, and Apple is no longer the youthful underdog. It's the symbol of technological conformity. Its market capitalisation is more than USD$3 trillion, and in Australia, more than half of all smartphones are Apple iPhones.[11] For many young people in Western nations in particular, the freedom to choose a smartphone is limited to the choice of colours between iPhones and Samsung phones. In Australia, Apple and Samsung have around 80% of the smartphone market share.[12] It seems that our hunger for acceptance and belonging surpasses our hunger for unconstrained freedom.

The road from unconstrained freedom – through technology – to uniformity comes with another side effect, the risk of stifling creativity. Twenty-six years after Apple coined its lead slogan 'Think different', a 2024 video advertisement for a new iteration of Apple's iPad demonstrated the

---

[11] Statcounter, *Mobile vendor market share Australia Oct 2023– Oct 2024*, GlobalStats website, November 2024, accessed 3 December 2024. https://gs.statcounter.com/vendor-market-share/mobile/Australia
[12] Ibid.

4. The Trap

industrial crushing of a pile of creative instruments – everything from painting easels and graphic design equipment to guitars and sound mixers. When everything had been crushed, all that was left was the iPad. It was a jarring symbol of the dehumanising and homogenising tendencies of technology. The more we look to technology to make us free, the more we risk trading away something of what it is to be human. It's a reminder of the ever-present risk that our technology can surpass and subsume our humanity.

The risk of ignoring the drift into mindless uniformity is also borne out in the field of behavioural economics, which seeks to make sense of the factors and trends that influence human decision-making. Social psychologist Solomon Ash conducted a series of experiments that found that even when free to judge, comment and decide for themselves on particular events, people are heavily influenced by the decisions and comments of those around them. Ash's findings have been replicated and extended in more than 130 subsequent experiments in 17 countries.[13] Could it be that we are built for conformity more fundamentally than we are built for freedom?

---

[13] Richard H Thaler and Cass R Sunstein, *Nudge: improving decisions about health, wealth, and happiness*, Penguin Books, London, 2009, p 60.

Again and again, when we are given the choice to do whatever we want, we end up deciding to want the same thing as those around us. This is borne out in our fast food, fast fashion, Netflix viewing data and Spotify streaming trends. Surely this tendency to uniformity is not accidental. If you threw 100 floating objects into different parts of a vast ocean, and they all drifted to the same place, you would assume that something beyond blind chance was at play. Clearly, there are currents. So what are the currents that keep dragging us to the same places? How has our individualism become so cloaked by collectivism?

British journalist and author Johann Hari writes of his experience with Ozempic®, an anti-obesity drug that suppresses the appetite. In an essay published in the *New York Times*, he cites a study that found that ultra-processed food made up 67% of what American children eat.[14] I suspect the equivalent statistic in other Western nations would reflect similar findings. Importantly, this kind of food makes people want to eat more and more, failing to satiate human hunger. Neuroscientists have confirmed this effect, finding that ultra-

---

[14] Johann Hari, 'Obesity, weight-loss drugs and ultraprocessed foods', *New York Times*, 19 May 2024, accessed 20 May 2024. https://www.nytimes.com/2024/05/19/opinion/obesity-weight-loss-drugs-ozempic.html

4. The Trap

processed diets leave our systems struggling to recognise healthy food as food at all, leaving us constantly craving more and more processed food. It helps explain why more people die globally today from eating too much than from having too little food. We are the first generations in human history for whom this is the case. Put another way, cutting-edge food-processing technology and limitless dietary options available to the global middle class are a trap. They are a jarring example of how just one industry has altered our appetites, leaving us wanting more of what they're selling.

Meanwhile, the pharmaceutical industry – exemplified by so-called wonder drugs like Ozempic® – responds to the market opportunity and offers to release us from *that* trap with a pill. In doing so, we play into another trap, that of an idealised body image. Both traps are offered as 'freedom' but are underpinned by inescapable markers of success. First, the ideal of having affordable, enjoyable food choices readily available without limits. Second, the ideal of ostensible physical health and social attractiveness. In Hari's words, 'we are trapped in a set of old stories.'[15] We seem to be drifting constantly between different measures of success, awash with choices but trapped by social expectations. It's almost as if a

15 Hari, 'Obesity'.

person's perpetually ballooning and contracting weight is part of some consumption pendulum that keeps our economy ticking.

A few years ago, my family and I travelled to Kuching, a small city on the island of Borneo in Malaysia. In many senses, we found what we expected. The wild orangutans of the jungle, the authentic eastern Malaysian cuisine on offer at countless waterfront restaurants and some of the friendliest people you could imagine. All of this was wonderful, but not unexpected. The moment that really struck me was when we were driving past a nondescript, beaten-down shopping strip. It had a few cafes, a hairdresser and a couple of other speciality stores. But the names of the stores were telling: Motown Bar and Bistro. Snoop café and the New American Taylor. It got me thinking about how measures of success are increasingly conditioned and standardised. This was a little Malaysian island thousands of kilometres from the United States. And yet, small businesses there sought to model their image on very specific touchpoints in American subculture. Sure, some of it could be to appeal to Western tourists. However, the number of American tourists who visit Kuching is dwarfed by tourists from other parts of Malaysia and from within Asia. To me, it was a signal that even in developing countries, measures and markers of success are increasingly uniform.

And it's not just about American cultural power. When we got back to Singapore after that trip – where we were living at the time – I began to see these common cultural touchpoints of success everywhere. Apartment complexes in Singapore named Casablanca, Manhattan and The Santorini. And it wasn't just Singapore. The growing ubiquity of Western fashion labels in Indian cinema. Africa's most admired brands are Nike, Adidas, Samsung, Coca Cola and Apple.[16] The most recognised brands in China include Apple and Samsung.[17] Even in the authoritarian theocracy of Iran, where Western brands and companies are widely prohibited, fast-food options named Pizza Hat, Mash Donald's and ZFC speak to a globalised consumer culture.[18] And if you happen to be in

---

[16] Citizen Reporter, *Nike, Adidas, Samsung top list of most admired brands in Africa,* Citizen Digital website, 9 August 2023, accessed 15 June 2024. https://www.citizen.digital/news/nike-adidas-samsung-top-list-of-most-admired-brands-in-africa-n325218

[17] Robynne Tindall, *What are the top ten brands in China?,* Soledad website, 18 August 2021, accessed 23 July 2024. https://focus.cbbc.org/what-are-the-top-ten-brands-in-china/amp/amp/

[18] Alireza Alizadeh, *What are the top Iranian brands?,* American Marketing Association New York, website, n.d., accessed 20 July 2024. https://www.amanewyork.org/resources/what-are-the-top-iranian-brands-iranian-brand-experts-insight/

Palestine or China and feel like a cappuccino, your options include 'Stars and Bucks' or 'Bucks-stars Coffee'. Ring any bells?

In a world where measures of success are standardised, even the ideal of individuality can lead to uniformity. When groups of people are motivated and influenced by similar forces, they begin to think, sound and behave like each other. From biker gangs to finance bros, hippies to hipsters, gamers to skaters, and surfers to triathletes, the human quest for uniqueness and nonconformity often ends up with people thinking, looking, sounding and acting in similar ways. Could it be that the proliferation of digital technology – and all that comes with it – has us all slowly morphing into one giant blob of monolithic cultural expression, shaped by modern ideas of success?

Edward Bernays, the nephew of seminal psychoanalyst Sigmund Freud and godfather of modern marketing, recognised the unifying influence of advertising on our choices. He observes that a man buying a suit may assume he is choosing something based on his taste and personality, but he is obeying the ideas and wishes of the design tailor, the manufacturer and the fashion media of the day.[19] We're increasingly

---

19 Edward Bernays, *Propaganda*, IG Publishing, New York,

4. The Trap

thinking, acting, streaming and buying in similar ways from similar places. It all represents a globalisation and homogenisation of consumer culture. As the political philosopher John Gray contends, our reward centres are built by forces that we don't control.[20]

Our consumer options are primed by the world around us. They reflect the collective agreement of society on the markers of success. As buyers, users and accumulators of stuff, we have more choices than ever before. However, the nature and number of those choices are the result of a centuries-old market-driven process that has left a surprisingly small number of corporate giants deciding what we get to choose from. As per automotive tycoon Henry Ford, a customer could have any colour they want, as long as it was black![21] Today, you can do whatever you want, provided that the communities from which you seek meaning and identity deem it normal, desirable, fashionable and acceptable.

1955, pp 61–62.

[20] John Gray, *Straw dogs: thoughts on humans and other animals*, Penguin Books, London, 2002.

[21] B Sullivan, *Any color the customer wants, as long as it's black*, James Madison Museum of Orange County Heritage website, 15 February 2023, accessed 7 November 2024. https://www.thejamesmadisonmuseum.net/single-post/any-color-the-customer-wants-as-long-as-it-s-black-henry-ford

We can't help but want to be successful, and though we get to choose a lot of things, we tend to accept our society's idea of what 'success' looks like. As the late Harvard University economist Theodore Levitt puts it, 'The world's needs and desires have been irrevocably homogenized.'[22] Freedom is supposed to liberate, but somehow we've built a world in which it totalises. We were told that it's all about being our best selves. But perhaps it's more accurately about all of us striving towards being a particular kind of best self – one that buys, watches and listens to similar things. As one economist put it: 'The products and methods of the industrialized world play a single tune for all the world, and all the world eagerly dances to it.'[23]

We all think of success in the same way. It's like someone's given us the keys to the car of our dreams, but they have told us that we're only allowed to drive it to one place. If we're effectively coerced into pointing our freedom at a predetermined set of 'success' markers, how free are we?

---

[22] Theodore Levitt, 'The globalization of markets', *Harvard Business Review*, May 1983, accessed 3 September 2024. https://hbr.org/1983/05/the-globalization-of-markets
[23] Ibid.

4. The Trap

Trapped by technology

Educator and cultural critic Neil Postman thought that our misunderstanding of freedom can be put down to some kind of over-correction. We're so focused on throwing off limits that we're 'amusing ourselves to death.'[24] To make his point, Postman unpacked two versions of fictional dystopia – each one depicted by a science-fiction writer from the 20th century. The first was George Orwell's famous novel *1984*, which tells of a society with a totalitarian, all-controlling government that monitors everything and everyone. It's where we got the phrase 'Big Brother', but unlike the reality TV show, no one gets to leave the 'house'.

In stark contrast to Orwell's authoritarian dystopia, there stands another dystopia crafted by author Aldous Huxley in his novel *Brave New World*. Preceding Orwell's work by around 17 years, Huxley's story is set in a futuristic world-state where people are artificially engineered into a social hierarchy based on intelligence. In this world, citizens are kept pain-free and peaceful by being constantly administered a happiness-inducing drug called 'soma'. In this society of

---
[24] Neil Postman, *Amusing ourselves to death,* Methuen Publishing, North Yorkshire, 1987.

meaningless numbness, civilisation itself is a process of pacifying. Sound any alarm bells? Huxley's prediction echoes a lot of the research around the effects of technology today. According to Postman, '[Huxley] believed that it is far more likely that the Western democracies will dance and dream themselves into oblivion than march into it, single file and manacled.'[25]

Our freedom-centric instincts have always railed against the idea of Big Brother. We even fought a 50-year Cold War over it. From Dr. Seuss's *Yertle the turtle* to modern democratic constitutions, we run from even the mild possibility of ending up in anything like Orwell's *1984*. However, as we bolt from the clutches of Big Brother, are we unwittingly running into the soft tranquilisation of Huxley's escapism?

Two of the great drivers and shapers of the modern world are capitalism and technology. We love making stuff, buying stuff and using stuff that makes life easier. The implied messages that we soak in tell us that we are, first and foremost, consumers. Techno-consumerism has given us everything from indoor plumbing and electricity to smartphones and smart fridges. But what has it taken away? As we browse, click and stream our way through life, we think less and less about

[25] Ibid., p 113.

4. The Trap

what freedom is and what freedom is for. And when you think less and less about something, eventually, you cede control of it. Like a happily oblivious swimmer caught in a rip at the beach, we're drifting with the currents of techno-capitalism and everything that goes with it, for better and worse.

The power of technology is bringing us together in more ways than we think – good and bad. Techno-consumerism guarantees the best things at the lowest prices based on the best technology that we have. There is more stuff around than ever before. Stuff we buy. Stuff we watch. Stuff we stream. Stuff we listen to. Yes, all of this improves our quality of life in some ways. But our technology-driven consumer lifestyles can also herd us, distract us and coerce us.

Tech expert and author Andy Crouch explains that technology always makes new things possible that were previously impossible, but it also makes some things impossible (or at least less likely) that were previously possible.[26] Video calls are great for connecting with people far away from us in real-time. However, they also make it less likely that we'll sit down for a coffee with a colleague on a different floor in our office block

---

[26] Andy Crouch, *Culture making: recovering our creative calling*, InterVarsity Press, Downers Grove, 2008, p 27.

when we can just jump on Zoom or Teams for a quick virtual chat.

Research suggests that the average modern consumer takes in as much as 74 gigabytes of information a day through TV, computers, mobile phones, tablets, billboards and other forms of input. This is the equivalent of watching 16 movies per day. Just a few hundred years ago, this daily amount of information intake would have been what a highly educated person consumed in a lifetime, mainly through books and stories.[27] A fair chunk of our time spent digesting information is – unsurprisingly – from social media, with the average person spending around 2.5 hours per day doom-scrolling.[28] Our attempts to digest something meaningful from the relentless images, posts, words, songs and videos coming at us make good conditions for input indigestion.

We're drinking from a firehose, and we're struggling to control the water pressure. As Johann Hari suggests in his book *Stolen Focus*, the

---

[27] Sabine Heim and Andreas Keil, *Too much information, too little time: how the brain separates important from unimportant things in our fast-paced media world,* frontiers website, 1 June 2017, accessed 11 November 2024. https://kids.frontiersin.org/articles/10.3389/frym.2017.00023

[28] Simon Kemp, *The time we spend on social media,* Datareportal website, 31 January 2024, accessed 25 October 2024. https://datareportal.com/reports/digital-2024-deep-dive-the-time-we-spend-on-social-media

4. The Trap

modern social-media landscape is intentionally designed to pull you away from your own life and keep you on apps for as long as possible, with a view to showing you more advertisements.[29] While experiences of technology undoubtedly vary from person to person, the massive ad revenues these companies pull in seem to indicate that their business model is working. But is it working for you and me?

The more the system knows about us, the better it gets at tailoring our experience to our preferences and desires. Things are easier to find, buy, understand and access. That's a good thing. However, this is not always happening on our terms, and certainly not independently of broader invisible motives. The more anyone knows about you, the better equipped they are to get you to do what they want you to do. And the more that happens, the less authentic your freedom is. Harvard Professor Shoshana Zuboff says that when we buy into the full-scale technological consumer lifestyle of digital living, we do it with the desire to exercise control over our lives, 'but everywhere that control is thwarted [and] we become the means to others' ends.'[30]

---

[29] Johann Hari, *Stolen focus*, Bloomsbury Publishing, London, 2022, pp 101–137.

[30] Shoshana Zuboff, *The age of surveillance capitalism: the*

In her book *No Logo*, journalist Naomi Klein writes about the curious concept known as 'synergy nirvana'.[31] It happens when a company's different divisions are integrated into a seamless whole so that each division uses the others to boost profits across the organisation. Think of Disney using its theme parks, T-shirts, TV channels and record labels to market its movies. Think of Apple's acquisition of Beats by Dre in 2014, bringing Beats' popular headphones and streaming service into Apple's ecosystem. These moves can make for positive experiences for the consumer. For example, Facebook's (now Meta's) acquisition of Instagram in 2012 has made for a much smoother and more integrated user experience between the two platforms. But it also makes it far less likely that we'll switch out of either social network. The deeper we go in, the more entrenched we become. In tech, as in life, our choices lead to fewer choices. Klein summarises it as a carnival on the surface but consolidation underneath.[32]

When corporate synergy goes up, consumer choice goes down. We hear more and more from fewer and fewer voices. As a result, we are

---

fight for a human future at the new frontier of power, Ingram Publisher Services, La Vergne, 2017, p 49.
[31] Naomi Klein, *No logo*, 4th Estate GB, London, 2010, ch 8.
[32] Ibid., ch 4.

4. The Trap

increasingly trapped by a smaller and smaller group of companies that we get our stuff from. From the suburbs of Sydney to the streets of Shanghai to the schoolyards of Rome, it's easy to find people carrying iPhones, sporting similar fashion, streaming similar Spotify playlists or watching Netflix, all while browsing the Amazon catalogue. We're swept up in a global consumer monoculture – some have called it 'Coca-Colanisation.'[33] On one level, we're exercising enormous amounts of freedom, but all the while we are still beholden to our Nikes, Netflix accounts and Nespresso machines.

Our viewing habits, reading habits, shopping habits and listening habits are carefully examined by the algorithms that run our digital worlds. As a result, we are quietly herded into virtual silos where we feel most comfortable. We are surrounded by those who agree with us; offered the products and experiences that we're used to; and closed off from ideas, information and, perhaps most damagingly, people from outside of our tribes. Our digital lives leave us more connected to the products, people and ideologies that naturally resonate

---

[33] Mark Pendergrast, 'A brief history of Coca-Colonization', *The New York Times*, 15 August 1993, accessed 11 November 2024. https://www.nytimes.com/1993/08/15/business/viewpoints-a-brief-history-of-coca-colonization.html

with us and close us off from everything else. This fragmentation has chewed away at aspects of our common human experience. On an average Thursday evening in the 1990s, more people watched any episode of the sitcom *Seinfeld* than the number of people who watched the highly anticipated finale of *Game of Thrones* in 2019. Midweek middle-class television habits might seem trivial, but they reflect the reality that there is less and less that we do together as a society.

Our tech-driven world has also contributed to at least a part of a growing mental health crisis in developed countries. The largest-ever global study into youth mental health identifies unregulated social media, global instability and tech-related anxieties as key contributing causes of the deteriorating mental health of young people. Astonishingly, almost 50% of Australian women aged between 16 and 24 report experiencing a mental health disorder.[34] One commented, 'I think the reason why this crisis is getting worse and worse is to do with the world that we are set to inherit.'[35] For all of its benefits, a world built on

---

34 Patrick D McGorry et al., 'The *Lancet Psychiatry* Commission on youth mental health', *The Lancet Psychiatry*, 2024, 11(9):731–774, accessed 15 August 2024. https://www.thelancet.com/commissions/youth-mental-health

35 Rachel Carbonell and Rhiannon Hobbins, *Youth mental health is a 'global crisis' according to world-leading study*,

the promises of freedom and technology alone is clearly not enough.

Whether it's the choices we struggle with, the consequences we deal with, the success we aspire to or the stuff we want, freedom can trap us as easily as it liberates us. In fact, the tricky reality is that it seems to be doing both at the same time. Somehow, the fruits of freedom don't always have the taste of freedom. When our central motivation is to throw off constraints, the type of freedom we get is one that totalises – trapping us in our choices, consequences, desires and our longing to fit in. Surely there's another way.

ABC News website, 14 August 2024, accessed 17 August 2024. https://www.abc.net.au/news/2024-08-14/global-teen-mental-health-study-urges-action/104218614

Re:CONSIDERING

5. ESCAPING THE FREEDOM TRAP

The picture I've painted might seem pessimistic. What's wrong with a few extra Tim Tam options and saving some travel time with video calls? Should I just lighten up? Maybe. But I think a few small tweaks to how we understand freedom can make a big difference – for the better.

First of all, it's worth re-affirming that while modern freedom might not be perfect, it's far better than its nasty social and political alternatives: restriction, oppression, subjugation and a host of other ugly words that end in 'ion'. I'm not suggesting that we do away with the freedom project just because it has a few bugs in it. However, the 'freedom trap', as I've set it out – catalysed by choice for its own sake, the unconsidered consequences of our choices, predetermined notions of success and restrictive aspects of technology – calls for a course correction. I'm pretty sure it's not time to throw the baby out with the bathwater. But it's probably time to think about why the baby's in there in the first place. Can we frame our freedom in such a way that we still get to enjoy choice and technology while pursuing happiness and success, without being entrapped and enframed? Perhaps there's some ancient wisdom that can blast us out of modern freedom's trappings. First, we need to be clear on the difference between 'freedom' and 'autonomy.'

The challenge of autonomy

Our modern freedom project might be better understood as a drift from the freedom-loving individual to the autonomy-seeking individual. The difference between freedom and autonomy is something that's relevant to all of us, not just political and moral philosophers. The idea of being free was largely about not being oppressed and being able to do what we wanted. However, 'autonomy' goes a step further. It seems to suggest that we should not only be able to choose to do what we want, but also choose for ourselves what constitutes a 'good' choice, free of all traditions and standards outside of ourselves. The iconic words of John Stuart Mill – one of the

5. Escaping the Freedom Trap

grandfathers of liberalism – sum it up. Writing of the individual, he declares: 'Over himself, over his own body and mind, the individual is sovereign.' He's not writing about mere freedom. He's writing about autonomy.[1] It sounds like a pretty good deal. And in many ways, it is. To a degree, we are wired for autonomy. The ability to choose – free of constraints – is inextricably linked to human dignity. But is there more to the story?

From the Greek words *auto* (self) and *nomos* (law), a truly autonomous person is a law unto themselves. A free person can drive their car anytime they want, but an autonomous person can drive it at whatever speed they want, without a seatbelt, regardless of limits, logic or the safety of others. While most people would agree that full-scale autonomy is neither practical nor desirable, it's the message that we often hear if we listen carefully to the drumbeat of modern consumer culture.

In his revolutionary anthem *Imagine,* 20th-century pop icon John Lennon offered a skeleton of what true autonomy might look like. He proclaimed the need for a world without countries, possessions or religion, where people would be united in peace and harmony. For Lennon, the

---

[1] John Stuart Mill, *On liberty*, Penguin Books, Middlesex, 1974, p 69.

ancient idea of 'the good life' *is* the problem. People shouldn't have right and wrong imposed upon them. For Lennon and his contemporaries, the answer was to get rid of first principles. According to Lennon, what we need is freedom underpinned by autonomy, not freedom constrained by dogma. At first glimpse, it's a nice thought. And there is much of what Lennon stood for that we would do well to remember – the longing for peace, human equality and nonviolent means to resolve conflict. However, the longing to eliminate constraints also contains a glaring contradiction. Lennon's vision of a world without first principles is – it turns out – packed with first principles. Peace is good. Harmony is good. Greed and hunger are bad. I agree with all of these principles, but they *are* principles. They all represent constraints – ideals that require the curtailing of various freedoms. Implicit in this freedom-unlimited vision of the world is a very precise idea of what is good, what the 'good life' is and what a 'good society' is, and it calls for all kinds of limits.

Something modern society continues to grapple with – and that Lennon warned against – is religion. At least some of the modern search for freedom has been driven – or at least accompanied by – a relative decline in those identifying with it. While the number of people with religious beliefs

5. Escaping the Freedom Trap

continue to grow globally, Western democracies have seen a relative decline in those who identify with organised religion. The idea of God – according to some – represents another set of constraints to throw off so we can live our best lives and be our best selves. Studies of those who have walked away from a former religious faith report liberation as an important motivator in their decision to renounce their faith. However, those same people also reported that a renunciation of faith in the name of freedom came with a sense of loss in relation to their former lifestyles and communities.[2] Then there are others – people who proudly proclaim their faith – who claim a far deeper sense of freedom than they had before they believed. On at least one side of the faith fence, there seems to be an incorrect – or at least incomplete – understanding of what true freedom is. Some walk away from God in the name of freedom. Others seek God and, as the Bible claims, find deeper freedom through their faith.[3]

The poet and writer Archibald MacLeish defined conquest as the dictation of behaviour. If he's right, to work out whether someone, something or some idea has conquered you, all you have to do is take a

---

[2] John Marriot, *The anatomy of deconversion*, ACU Press, Abilene, 2020, pp 153–167.
[3] John 8:36.

good look at whether or not it's dictating how you behave.[4] On this measure, it's pretty clear that our march towards autonomy is not so much about the 'good life' but about a life without limits of any kind. Our well-intentioned search for freedom may be leading us to be conquered by an incomplete understanding of freedom. Our modern societies have been conquered by the idea that true freedom is about throwing off all constraints.

When freedom isn't understood healthily, we can become buried under our choices, victims of the consequences of our choices or pressured into making choices that fit with social markers of success over which we have no control. Whether bombarding ourselves with varieties of jam, unconsciously submitting to the demands of our smartphones or ignoring the consequences of our choices, the drift into autonomy may be where we've lost our way. Part of what gets missed is that there's never fully-fledged autonomy. It seems that there's no way around the reality that we're always beholden to constraints in some way.

In modern attempts to emancipate ourselves from some of our ancient ideals, we seem to have merely bought into a new deal. Some have claimed

---

[4] Archibald MacLeish, 'The conquest of America', *The Atlantic*, August 1949, accessed on 11 November 2024. https://www.theatlantic.com/magazine/archive/1949/08/the-conquest-of-america/643183/

5. Escaping the Freedom Trap

that God is dead, but there doesn't seem to be a shortage of new gods on offer. Equipped with our smartphones, smart homes, online shopping accounts and livestream subscriptions, we haven't so much eliminated constraints as much as we've switched from old constraints to new constraints.

To fill the vacuum, we have elevated new objects of worship: our national identities,[5] the power of our global markets,[6] our hunger for pleasure and entertainment[7] or – as I've already explored – our pursuit of the modern markers of success.[8] Perhaps we have replaced traditional places of worship with new ones – gyms, football stadiums, shopping centres, restaurants and clubs. We can't seem to stop being religious. All that's shifting around is what we're religious about.

One way or another, it seems impossible to escape the reality that we're always conquered by something. It might seem unsettling, but what if our millennia-old search for freedom points to the increasingly clear reality that freedom from everything is not possible? There is always an invisible Wizard of Oz – sometimes theistic,

---

[5] William T Cavanaugh, *Migrations of the holy: God, state, and the political meaning of the church*, Eerdmans Publishing, Grand Rapids, 2011, pp 7–45.

[6] Gray, *The new leviathans*, ch 3.

[7] Postman, *Amusing ourselves to death,* pp 110–120.

[8] Gray, *Straw dogs*.

sometimes atheistic – behind the curtain and pulling the strings. The animals in George Orwell's classic story *Animal Farm* revolt against their human carers, only to mindlessly submit themselves to oppression by the pigs. The question then is not about whether constraints are good or bad, but rather, it is about what the right kinds of constraints are. The Bible puts it pretty bluntly, declaring that we are all slaves to whatever has mastered us.[9]

18th-century jurist Alexander Fraser Tytler suggested that human society tends to go through eight civilisational cycles. From bondage to spiritual faith; from spiritual faith to courage; from courage to liberty; from liberty to abundance, from abundance to selfishness; from selfishness to apathy, from apathy to dependency; and from dependency back to bondage once more.[10] It seems a bit simplistic. But a quick glance at the world around us suggests that Tytler's ideas are worth a look. There are undeniable resonances with the idea of liberty and abundance (e.g. democracy, human rights, industrial revolutions, digital technology and modern medicine). More

---

[9] 2 Peter 2:19.
[10] Henning W Prentis, 'The cult of competency', *The General Magazine and Historical Chronicle*, University of Pennsylvania, The General Alumni Society, April 1943, XLV(III).

worryingly, modern struggles with individualism, anxiety, polarisation and addiction seem to chime with Tytler's warnings against selfishness, apathy and dependency. At least on some level, the way we've understood and used our liberty seems to have nudged us into the negative second half of the cycle. Interestingly, the 'recovery' phase – according to Tytler at least – has to do with what we believe in.

British podcaster and writer Justin Brierley has suggested – using both qualitative and quantitative data – that there has been a surprising swing back towards faith and spirituality.[11] Perhaps the trends that Brierley and others have noticed suggest that some of our newfound 'gods' haven't been all we'd hoped. If that's true, the answer may well be – according to Brierley, Tytler and others – a renewed commitment to finding the right constraints to re-rail our freedom project to target something beyond freedom, and perhaps something beyond ourselves.

---

[11] Justin Brierley, *The surprising rebirth of belief in God: why new atheism grew old and secular thinkers are considering Christianity again*, Tyndale Elevate, Carol Stream, 2024.

Re-imagining the 'good life'

There is a debate among political and moral theorists sometimes referred to as the 'Freedom From' vs 'Freedom to' debate. It's an old and complicated debate – with many sub-factions and disagreements both between and within each side – but this dichotomy has had a big say in how people have been trying to make sense of freedom for at least the last 3,000 years.

The Freedom-from camp contends that throwing off constraints and limits is enough in itself. For such thinkers, there's no better life than a life without limits lived on one's own terms. The Freedom-for camp takes a different view. They believe that the gradual elimination of limits is not enough. Yes, we should be free of the wrong kind of constraints, but the way we set up our societies should also reflect some agreed common aspiration and direction. Some have called it the 'good life.'

When we consider some of the trappings of freedom – as I've briefly catalogued – it's pretty clear that they all find fertile soil in the world thought up by the Freedom-from team. From philosophers John Stuart Mill and Jean Jacques

5. Escaping the Freedom Trap

Rousseau to Frank Sinatra's 'My Way' to the modern hashtags #YouDoYou and #YourBestSelf, the Freedom-from camp has plenty of runs on the board in its influence on modern life.

The blind spot of the Freedom-from camp seems to be its neglect of the nature and purposes of the constraints that they're throwing off. The project can escalate into the idea of freedom for its own sake. Referring to the artist movement in Germany in the 1920s known as the Bauhaus movement, the writer and commentator Tom Wolfe explored some of the pitfalls in trying to eliminate all norms and restraints of the past and starting out from zero. The idea behind the Bauhaus movement was to sweep aside all architectural styles of the past and create a new style that was not beholden to anything that came before – free of the dead hand of the past.[12] The design tradition continues to have its adherents. However, according to Wolfe, by the late 1970s, many architects were complaining about the dead hand of the Bauhaus – flat leaky roofs, tiny beige office cubicles and sterile facades.[13] Good architecture, it seems, needs to draw on something

---

12 Tom Wolfe, 'The great relearning', *The American Spectator*, 1987, 20(12):14, accessed 20 October 2024. https://www.unz.com/print/AmSpectator-1987dec-00014
13 Ibid.

of its own history to get past the limiting idea of freedom for its own sake. As liberating as it might sound, starting from zero doesn't seem to work.

In 2011, at least nine countries were directly affected by the Arab Spring – a large-scale movement of democratic protests across North Africa and the Middle East. They didn't all work out, but some of them toppled long-standing authoritarian governments, including that of Egypt. The famous Egyptian protest chant that captured the essence of the movement was 'bread, freedom, human dignity'.[14] Their longings went beyond the symbolic political desire for freedom. They wanted – they needed – more than that. The addition of bread and dignity as objectives of the movement spoke to the felt need for more than the mere absence of oppression. Material needs and a sense of worth and wellbeing were – for most protestors – at least as important as freedom from authoritarian government control. The message was clear: freedom is a good start, but it's not enough.

Around 3,000 years earlier, another uprising occurred in the Middle East just down the road

---

[14] Killian Clarke, *'Aish, huriyya, karama insaniyya*: framing and the 2011 Egyptian uprising', *European Political Science* 2013, 12:197–214, accessed 11 November 2024. https://link.springer.com/article/10.1057/eps.2012.41

from Cairo's Tahrir Square, which was ground zero for Egypt's Arab Spring protests. Around the 13th century BC, the people of the nation of Israel escaped from more than 300 years of slavery under the might of the ancient Egyptian empire. It's the most dramatic account of liberation depicted in the Bible, even justifying a book named for this single event – Exodus. The word 'exodus' was adopted into English from the Greek word *exodos*, which means 'the road out'. For the ancient Israelites, as for the modern Egyptians, a road out of oppression begs the follow-up question: the road out to where?

In Disney's hit cartoon film *The Prince of Egypt* – which tells of Ancient Israel's liberation from slavery – the final montage during which the people of Israel are marching out of Egypt is accompanied by a song from earlier in the movie that is now sung in Hebrew. As you'd expect, the song includes a declaration of their freedom from slavery. Sure, that seems simple enough. However, the chant doesn't end with freedom. The people of Israel also cry out for healing. Their celebration of freedom is underpinned by the need for more than freedom. Their cry for healing suggests that freedom is not simply a set of constraint-free environmental conditions but a means to something else. The implication is that freedom for its own sake is not enough. The people wanted and needed more than the absence of oppression. They were – as we are – looking for a more holistic and multi-dimensional kind of wellbeing than mere political freedom. We long for bread. We long for dignity. We long for wellbeing. Freedom is part of the 'good life', but it isn't an end in itself.

For the people of Israel and for billions of others since – who identify with the Judeo-Christian tradition – this notion of complete wellbeing is often referred to as 'shalom', meaning holistic peace and fullness of health and blessing. It recognises that even in the most epic of liberation stories, freedom was not an end in itself. People need more than the absence of constraints.

In July 1983, my father and I were trapped in a locked bathroom just south of the CBD of Sri Lanka's capital city, Colombo. Outside was a vicious death squad of government-sanctioned thugs, trying to break the lock and attack us – with the intention of killing us. They were drugged, enraged and equipped with various weapons. We weren't the only family attacked, but as Tamils living in Colombo, we represented the primary targets of the horror that is now known as 'Black July' – perhaps the worst month in Sri Lanka's tragic 50-year civil war. Tamils were brutally attacked, tortured and killed across the country. By

5. Escaping the Freedom Trap

what can only be described as a series of miracles, my parents and I survived that night, though we had to watch our home and possessions burn to the ground while hiding in nearby bushes. We escaped Colombo soon after on a cargo ship to the north of the country, where we took refuge until we were offered Humanitarian Refugee status by the Australian Government, through a special visa program initiated personally by then Australian Prime Minister Bob Hawke.

My parents told me the harrowing story of our escape countless times. While growing up, I ran it over and over in my head, struggling with the injustice of it all while trying to organise for myself the duelling realities of all we'd been gifted alongside all that had been taken from us. As new Australians, we had been given the gifts of life and freedom. That much was clear. But it quickly became obvious that there was more to the story. My parents taught me that with our new freedom came responsibilities. The responsibility to honour the second chance at life we'd been given. The responsibility to live well, to live with purpose, to live with meaning and to work hard for the broader success of my new home country and her people. The freedom I had been afforded was not a license to do whatever I wanted but to have a decent crack at living in a way that I should.

I know it's easy to trip over that word – 'should' – these days. It's generally avoided as unnecessarily provocative, a red alert for a conversation that's at risk of slipping from the 'comfortable' into the 'ethical'. But I couldn't dodge it. Alongside our lives and our freedom, we had been gifted with a new shot at happiness, purpose and meaning. Having stared death in the face, we now stared down opportunity and community. There was no legal obligation to honour these responsibilities, but ignoring them left the question unanswered: Freedom for what?

I began travelling overseas for holidays, backpacking trips and university exchange programs, and I spent some time living and working overseas too. As is so often the case for people who travel abroad, every time I came home, I was grateful to be back. As I tried to unpack why this is such a common sentiment at the international arrival gates of airports, something struck me. For a country drenched in freedom and opportunity, Australia is replete with rules, laws, taxes, protocols, systems, standards and regulations. The gift of being Australian came – it turned out – wrapped in a decent measure of red tape. And while admittedly, some of it is unnecessary and much of it is annoying, it turned out that a lot of it was important. Yes, we came

5. Escaping the Freedom Trap

for freedom. But we also came to be safe, to be treated with respect, to own property, to receive healthcare, to be educated, to raise families, to make friends, to travel, to explore and to enjoy everything Australia has to offer. For these longings to be satisfied, certain constraints were – and are – essential.

Within minutes of turning 17, I wanted the freedom to drive a car. Any time there were school and university holidays, I wanted the freedom to travel. After getting my first few pay cheques, I began exploring the freedom of buying my first home. It became clear that these extra freedoms always came as a package deal – with accountability, responsibility and, importantly, constraints: laws; constitutions; taxes; police and emergency services; infrastructure like roads, rail and air traffic control; and of course, social standards of civility and decency (both legislated and unlegislated). These all enabled my personal freedom to work alongside the freedom of others in real life.

Two realities kept revealing themselves. Firstly, to be meaningfully free, people need constraints. Secondly, freedom needs to be pointed at something beyond itself. An Uber driver without a passenger and a destination is just a guy in a car. Unconstrained freedom leaves us without purpose. Unguided freedom leaves us scrambling for meaning. It turns out that emancipation only works if you're being emancipated from the right things and for the right things.

The idea of a 'good life' is an old one. The ancient Egyptians emphasised order. The ancient Chinese focused on social harmony. The ancient Greeks prioritised virtue. The ancient Indians and Mesopotamians valued the fulfilment of duties. While definitions varied, one thing that didn't was the idea that there *was* a common 'good life' to which people should aspire. It's an idea that was as common in ancient times as smartphones are today. However, it's an idea that's become increasingly foreign to the modern mind.

I admit that any attempt to direct anyone's freedom can – for a lot of reasons that go beyond the scope of this little book – seem oppressive. According to Google's *NGram* database, which tracks word use, the frequency of words like 'submit' and 'submission' has fallen off a cliff since 1996, reducing by more than 60%.[15] We have drifted, it seems, from seeking to conform our lives to a common idea of what is 'good' to trying to conform reality to our individual preferences of what we think is 'good'. The 'good life' has not

---

[15] Google Ngram viewer, search for 'submit', accessed 3 December 2024.

been thrown out, but our modern consumerist sensibilities have redefined it. Now, the 'good life' is whatever you want it to be. In throwing off constraints, have we lost sight of what freedom is supposed to be for?

Re:CONSIDERING

6. RECLAIMING FREEDOM

Purpose-driven freedom

Historian Yuval Noah Harari has summarised the freedom-centric approach to life as a modern contract in which 'humans agree to give up meaning in exchange for power.'[1] It echoes Neil Postman's insight that we trade our freedom for pleasure.[2] One way or another, we seem to be trading away important things to protect the idea that we can do whatever we want. But no matter how hard we try, we can't seem to get away from our need for more than a life without constraints. Dr Clay Routledge, director of the Human Flourishing Lab, explains that our need for meaning is more important than our need for freedom. He argues that we are 'an existential species … We don't just strive for survival. We

---
[1] Yuval Noah Harari, *Homo deus: a brief history of tomorrow*, Vintage Arrow, New York, 2017, pp 200–202.
[2] Postman, *Amusing ourselves to death,* pp 160–168.

strive for significance ... I think meaning in life is at the core of psychological freedom.'[3]

In the fictional classic *Robinson Crusoe*, Daniel Defoe writes of a traveller who finds himself on a seemingly deserted island, completely free of government, regulations, laws and even social expectations. He was – in theory, at least – free from conventional limits. However – as Polish politician Ryszard Legutko suggests, maybe this kind of 'absolute freedom' is not really what we're looking for.[4] A deserted island where we're free from the tax office might be technically as free as one can be, but what about electricity, running water, wi-fi and that thing that we so often struggle without – other people? As Legutko goes on to explain, this kind of absolute freedom 'runs counter to human nature, so much so that the prospect of having it fills us with dread [...] absolute freedom is loneliness.'[5] The worldwide hit reality TV series *Alone* places people in the wilderness on their own to fend for themselves. As you'd imagine, contestants are strong, resourceful, resilient and highly capable. However, even the

---

[3] Clay Routledge, *Meaning and the psychology of freedom*, Profectus website, 12 January 2023, accessed 12 November 2024. https://profectusmag.com/meaning-and-the-psychology-of-freedom/
[4] Ryszard Legutko, *The cunning of freedom: saving the self in an age of false idols*, Encounter Books, New York, 2021, pp 11–15.
[5] Ibid., p 12.

show's winners admit to dealing with loneliness and acknowledge the need for human connection.[6]

Neil Postman says that 'we do not measure a culture by its output of undisguised trivialities but by what it claims as significant.'[7] The problem is that we don't seem to have much of a marker for measuring significance except how we feel and what other people think. The perpetual volatility of both of these things leaves us with a pretty unstable foundation on which to build our lives unless we can find a clearer purpose at which to point our freedom.

The yearning for freedom goes beyond simply wanting to be free from governments that bear down on us with control and surveillance, inhibiting speech, thought, property rights, conscience and religion. It also goes to what we need – provision, food and a wider sense of wellbeing. When people think of freedom, we tend to think of it as both essential to and part of a 'better life'. For life to be meaningful, we need to use our freedom to choose things that bring meaning.

Freedom, it seems, is never an end in itself. It's always about something else – something we seek,

---

[6] Tim Ashelford, *Interview with Gina Chick from* Alone *Australia season 1*, We Are Explorers website, 1 November 2023, accessed 12 November 2024. https://weareexplorers.co/interview-with-gina-chick-alone-australia/

[7] Postman, *Amusing Ourselves to Death,* p 69.

revere or look up to. Put another way, as soon as we are free, we begin to worship something. And in a world of plain autonomy, that thing tends to be us. Harari says that we've become little gods who are limited by nothing. You'd be forgiven for taking this as a declaration of empowerment and encouragement. However, tellingly, Harari goes on to ask, 'Is there anything more dangerous than dissatisfied and irresponsible gods who don't know what they want?'[8] His insight implies something that much of our experience bears out. When we worship nothing but ourselves, we struggle. It seems no coincidence, then, that the biblical account of the Israelites' liberation from slavery in ancient Egypt was for nothing if not for something in particular. When Moses famously requested that Pharaoh let his people go, it was not an end in itself. It was so they could worship God.[9]

Sitting on an empty oval by myself might render me 'free' in a technical sense. But I'd much rather be on that oval with a group of friends, with a cricket pitch in place, boundary lines set and a casual game of weekend cricket underway, with – of course – all the necessary accompaniments of a firing BBQ and a fully stocked esky. Constraints, systems, directed activities and other people

---

[8] Yuval Noah Harari, *Sapiens: a brief history of humankind*, Harvill Secker, London, 2015, pp 415–416.
[9] Exodus 8:1.

6. Reclaiming Freedom

necessarily constrain our freedom, but they also provide things that we seem to need. We need people. We need meaning. We need purpose. Perhaps – as per the Christian pastor Timothy Keller – to have real freedom, we need to choose the right constraints.[10] This speaks to the Bible's understanding of 'true freedom' – not as a license to do whatever I want, but an opportunity to do what I can and should to bring about wellbeing and wholeness. There's that word 'should' again – one of the arch rivals of the word 'autonomy'. Telling us moderns that we 'should' do something can be like telling a politician to ignore opinion polls. Seemingly nonsensical. Probably futile. Certainly a long shot. Why? Largely because words like 'should' open the can on the idea that we might locate who we are and determine how we should live in something outside of ourselves. It shifts our centre of gravity from shorter-term desires and preferences to longer-term things that are less about me. And while I'm all for doing the right thing, the less about *me* life becomes, the higher my eyebrows are raised in suspicion.

---

[10] Timothy Keller, *The search for values* [audio], sermon, delivered at Redeemer Presbyterian Church, New York, Spotify. 17 October 1993, accessed 10 April 2024. https://open.spotify.com/episode/1hE7FCX8JsjSpQu2udStdE?si=8xh27YzmS_yPc4tWD5iEWA

However, the payoffs of looking beyond ourselves are worth a second look. Perhaps true freedom is even more liberating than modern autonomy. When we locate our sense of identity and meaning in something outside of ourselves – like friendships, families, jobs, marriages, clubs or sports teams – we agree to submit ourselves to the commitments of the friendships, the objectives of the company, the vows of the marriage, the rules of the game or the goals of the team. We also receive the benefits of being part of something greater than ourselves. We become connected to other people, a deeper identity and a greater purpose. Watching exactly what I want to watch on TV seems desirable, but compromising to watch something my whole family wants to watch unlocks the benefits of a family movie night – complete with junk food, snacks and the tangible joy of communal laughter.

American philosopher David Bentley Hart defines 'true freedom' as bringing our lives into harmony with the ultimate nature of reality. It's not just about doing whatever we want. It's about using our choices to lean into what we are made for. Like how a sculptor reveals the hidden form from a block of marble, truly free people use their choices to realise their true nature and purpose as

6. Reclaiming Freedom

it lines up with a divine design.[11] Freedom, then, is not so much about creating ourselves. Rather, it is about tapping into the reasons for which we were created in the first place.

The possibilities unleashed by this ancient biblical idea of 'true freedom' go well beyond the latest offerings of Netflix combined with the latest offerings from Ben & Jerry's. Robert Smalls was born into slavery in South Carolina in 1839. In the most fundamental way, he was not free. However, his life is a powerful (and inspiring) example of purpose-driven freedom in action – and though largely untold, one of my favourite stories in all of history. In the middle of the American Civil War, Smalls escaped from his slave master, stole a Confederate ship from Charleston Harbour, piloted it out of pro-slavery waters and handed it over to become a Union warship. It was an audacious act of defection. In the process, he freed himself, his family, and his crew and their families, and even drew the praise of then President Abraham Lincoln, who – in response to Smalls' escapade – accepted African-American soldiers into the Union Army. Not done yet, Smalls went on to become a state and national member of parliament, pioneering South Carolina's free and

---

[11] David Bentley Hart, *The experience of God: being, consciousness, bliss*, Yale University Press, New Haven, 2013, p 54.

compulsory school system and authoring several pieces of legislation during America's post-war reconstruction. For Robert Smalls, freedom was about much more than the absence of oppression. It was about using the freedom from oppression for other purposes. Freedom didn't end with the absence of constraints. That was just the beginning.

The ancient Jewish idea of 'shalom' suggests that 'true freedom' doesn't travel alone. It needs companions to ensure a fuller, deeper and richer life that ensures wellbeing. It suggests that freedom without meaning is not enough. There must be meaning beyond limitlessness. And *that* meaning best comes through relationships, community and purpose. The freedom of speech is only real if someone is listening. The freedom of time is only meaningful if we have fulfilling options through which to spend that time. The freedom of thought is only satisfying if those thoughts bring about something positive – either for me or for others. Freedom in its purest and most powerful form – it seems – is a bit like flowing water. It needs systems, directions and purposes to bring satisfaction. A thunderstorm might offer the maximal provision of water, but if I'm parched, a full glass of water is more satisfying, fulfilling and practical.

If this is all starting to sound a bit suffocating, I hear you. As I've already said, our natural instincts

6. Reclaiming Freedom

tend to shy away from anyone or anything that tries to tell us what to do. And humanity's sad history of oppression, subjugation and discrimination leaves us understandably skittish around the idea that anyone can be trusted to tell us how we should live our lives. The respected philosopher Jean-Paul Sartre echoed this sentiment as he declared, 'Once liberty has exploded in the soul of a man, the gods can do nothing against that man.'[12] It's a pretty clear and direct message. No one gets to tell me what to do! In light of these sentiments, the idea of a God who can help us direct our freedom can seem suspicious. In fact, a part of the modern freedom project is to reject any such idea of some overarching cosmic plan to which we should adhere and submit.

Interestingly, however, the Christian message claims that God himself embraced limitations. He stepped into the world as a person, submitting himself to the human realities of hunger, thirst, pain, grief, loss, loneliness and, ultimately, death. According to the Bible, whenever Jesus voluntarily embraced limits, he did so with a broader purpose in mind. He was playing the long game. It was more than mere humility. It was strategy. Strategy underpinned by purpose. Regardless of one's

---

[12] Jean-Paul Sartre, *The Flies*, in *Altona, Men Without Shadows, The Flies*, Penguin, London, 1962, Act 2.

beliefs, the evidence for a deeper and truer variety of freedom plays out in everything from the health benefits of committed monogamous relationships[13] to public policy challenges like prescription drug abuse.[14] Yes, we want to be free. But perhaps 'true freedom' is about submitting to the right kinds of constraints – be they relationships, friendships, communities, families, sports teams or the laws that govern our societies.

True freedom relies on finding the right constraints that point to the right purposes. So what are they, and how do we find them?

What's love got to do with it?

Apu is the lovable fictional convenience store owner from the long-running TV show *The Simpsons*. Upon seeing the rampant consumerism championed by his rival, the 'Monster Mart'

---

[13] GA Schuiling, 'The benefit and the doubt: why monogamy?', *Journal of Psychosomatic Obstetrics and Gynaecology*, 2003, 24(1):55–61.

[14] Carrington Clarke and Pheove Hosier, 'Oregon's drug decriminalisation experiment is being rolled back after three years of rising drug use', ABC News website, 28 May 2024, accessed 30 June 2024. https://www.abc.net.au/news/2024-05-28/oregon-drug-decriminalisation-junkies-streets-fentanyl/103871432

store, he grumpily remarks, 'Great selection and rock-bottom prices. But where is the love?'[15] It's a passing and easily forgotten cartoon moment, but it speaks to two infatuations of the modern mind and the tension between them. We love freedom. We also love love. But how do they relate to each other? Political philosopher George Grant suggests that 'art and love can only find their fulfilment in a vision of nature in opposition to our freedom.'[16] Grant is pointing to the need for freedom to be harnessed, guided and directed in particular ways if it is to bring about that which is beautiful.

An ongoing longitudinal study on adult development conducted by researchers at Harvard University found that the strength and depth of relationships are what keep people happy throughout their lives.[17] True 'shalom' isn't about freedom, pleasure, wealth or fame. It's about relationships. In his TED Talk 'What makes a good life?' – viewed more than 48 million times – the director of the study, Dr Robert

---

[15] 'Homer and Apu', *The Simpsons*, created by Matt Groening, season 5, episode 13, Gracie Films and 20th Century Fox Television, 1994.

[16] George Grant, *Philosophy in a mass age*, The Copp Clark Publishing Company, Toronto, 1966, pp 109–111.

[17] Meredith Goldstein, 'The good life apparently requires other people', *The Boston Globe*, 1 March 2023, accessed 12 November 2024. https://www.bostonglobe.com/2023/03/01/arts/good-life-apparently-requires-other-people/

Waldinger, declares that 'this is wisdom that's as old as the hills [...] The good life is built with good relationships.'[18] Love – according to the science – is a pretty important part of what it means to be human. Freedom might be the ideal on which we've built modern economies and constitutions. But love is the ideal that keeps pouring out in our literature, movies and music. From Shakespeare to Taylor Swift, love has been centrestage. But what does love have to do with freedom?

French sociologist Émile Durkheim developed the idea of *anomie* – referring to the breaking down of commonly held social standards and moral principles, which leads to a sense of disconnection and purposelessness. There's that word 'purpose' again. According to social psychologist Jonathan Haidt, when this happens, our communities get weaker, and people suffer. The more unguided autonomy we have as individuals, the weaker our communities become. As Haidt puts it, 'People who live only in networks, rather than communities, are less likely to thrive.'[19] One of his suggested

---

[18] Robert Waldinger, 'What makes a good life? Lessons from the longest study on happiness', TED, filmed November 2015, TED2015, video, accessed 3 December 2024. https://www.ted.com/talks/robert_waldinger_what_makes_a_good_life_lessons_from_the_longest_study_on_happiness?subtitle=en

[19] Jonathan Haidt, *The anxious generation: how the great rewiring of childhood is causing an epidemic of mental illness*, Allen Lane, Dublin, 2024, p 203.

6. Reclaiming Freedom

solutions is a return to shared sacred times, places and objects. Haidt declares himself to be an atheist but concedes that in trying to explain all of this, he can't help but use 'words and concepts from religion to understand the experience of life as a human being.'[20] Evolutionary biologist EO Wilson agrees, labelling human beings 'biophilic', meaning that we have an in-built urge to affiliate with other forms of life.[21] This explains our affinity for horse riding, bird training and inviting children, cats, dogs and every other imaginable creature into our homes. It also explains cities, neighbourhoods, friendship and team sports. It seems that – regardless of someone's religious beliefs – there is something about the human experience that is satisfied only by community and connection. And we are willing to trade away aspects of our freedom to get them. As creatures built for connection, our freedom seems inextricably linked to our responsibilities to others. It's why World War II concentration camp survivor Viktor Frankl declared that we should have built a 'Statue of Responsibility' next to the Statue of Liberty.[22]

Many disagree. Thinkers like Jean-Paul Sartre, who – though an atheist like Haidt – put forward

---

[20] Ibid., p 201.

[21] Ibid., p 214.

[22] Victor E Frankl, *Man's search for meaning*, Beacon Press, Boston, 2006, p 132.

a very different view of freedom. For Sartre, other people are not subjects for loving but objects who radically negate 'my' experience. Assuming this view, the only options I have – as summarised by author Christopher Watkin – are to enslave them to my interests or to be enslaved to theirs.[23] Sounds a bit grim, but it's an honest summary of where we end up if we follow the idea that my freedom, preferences and desires are unimpeachable. Just make sure that no one messes with your freedom, and if what you want or feel rubs up against what someone else wants or feels, make sure you win. From ancient political strategists like Machiavelli to moral philosophers like Ayn Rand to modern self-help authors like Robert Greene, this strand of thinking operates on a simple idea: freedom is all about power.

In stark contrast, St Paul – the apostle who called people to freedom through Christianity – also wrote a famous treatise on love.[24] He begins by talking about fairly simple aspects of love – that it is patient and kind. But then, things get a little grittier. He declares that love rejects evil, holds onto truth and protects that which it loves. For Paul, love binds, it holds, it preserves and it sacrifices. Paul's brand of love necessarily regulates

---
[23] Watkin, *Biblical critical theory*, pp 148–149.
[24] 1 Corinthians 13.

6. Reclaiming Freedom

and constrains freedom, but according to him, without it, nothing else really matters. According to Paul and the Bible's idea of love, without love on the table, freedom is pointless. The North African theologian St Augustine echoed this idea, declaring that our wills are not truly free until they are no longer enslaved to our vices.[25]

Pulitzer Prize-winning author Marilynne Robinson summarises how this version of love fits with the Bible's idea of freedom. At its centre is a call to freely live in the way that God designed us to live as a means to 'shalom' – loving and serving others – at the expense of our own desires, if necessary.[26] According to this stream of thinking, freedom is not about power. Freedom is about love. As the author Frederick Buechner puts it:

> to obey Love itself, which above all else wishes us well, leaves us the freedom to be the best and gladdest that we have it in us to become. The only freedom Love denies us is the freedom to destroy ourselves ultimately.[27]

Perhaps our freedom is not something to point at the world around us, but a set of opportunities

---

[25] St Augustine, *The city of God*, books XIII and XIV, Liverpool University Press, Liverpool, 2017, book XIV.
[26] Marilynne Robinson, *Reading Genesis*, Farrar, Straus and Giroux, New York, 2024, p.19.
[27] Frederick Buechner, *Beyond words*, HarperCollins, New York, 2004, p 120.

to contribute to the wellbeing of others. Maybe reclaiming freedom begins with the realisation that freedom begins with other people.

Reclaiming freedom in everyday life

A whirlwind tour of what freedom is and how it works has uncovered some of its trappings. The drift from ancient understandings of freedom – underpinned by duty, purpose and responsibility – has carried us into a world where freedom is about getting what we want when we want it – supposedly, a life without limits. In a fast-paced autonomy-promoting world, it's easy for us moderns to miss the traps that come with overwhelming choice, unavoidable consequences, modern notions of success and cutting-edge technology that can disable as much as it enables. Can freedom be recalibrated and reclaimed to avoid these traps? I'm confident that it can.

Freedom is undoubtedly a good thing. From the viral dance sensation that swept Iran to the timeless tales of Dr Seuss to the countless songs, movies and stories that carry the enduring human aversion to subjugation, being free from oppression is part of what makes us human.

6. Reclaiming Freedom

However, freedom never travels alone or in the abstract. There is always a context, and there are always constraints. Billionaires are constrained by countless decisions about how to spend, protect and grow their money. Celebrities are constrained by the perpetual need to please the public and maintain their fame. Employees are constrained by the responsibilities of their jobs. Employers are constrained by their profit targets. Politicians are constrained by public sentiment. Even dictators are constrained by tenuous realities and the adverse cultural, economic and social consequences of governing illegitimately and without the consent of their people. From kindergarten playgrounds to national parliaments, there is always a blend of freedom, limitations and consequences at play.

Freedom is finite. Freedom fluctuates. And freedom is never without context or consequence. Accordingly, as we become collectively capable of more and more, it's worth reminding ourselves – as individuals – that there's plenty that we can't control. The over-stressed, under-slept modern individual might be portrayed as Atlas, with the world on their shoulders, but great control doesn't necessarily accompany the great modern expectations of success and achievement.

We can, however, control how we respond to circumstances. Victor Frankl said, 'Everything can be taken from a man but one thing: the last of the human freedoms – to choose one's attitude in any given set of circumstances, to choose one's own way.'[28] Our choices matter, but we are never unlimited. We are always choosing in a constrained environment, and our choices bring on more constraints. The key, then, seems to be getting the constraints right.

As the Pulitzer Prize-winning master jazz musician Wynton Marsalis said, 'You need to have some restrictions in jazz. Anyone can improvise with no restrictions, but that's not jazz. Jazz always has some restrictions. Otherwise it might sound like noise.'[29] Like a train that needs tracks, a fish that needs water or a basketball game that needs rules, perhaps escaping the trappings of freedom requires us to do something a little counterintuitive – finding the right constraints. Structures, systems and constraints don't necessarily stand opposed to freedom. They can augment it. Child psychologists advise that children with regular routines and structures are more secure, have better self-regulation and are mentally healthier.[30] And it's

---

[28] Frankl, *Man's search for meaning*, p 86.

[29] Ayer, *The art of choosing*, p 214.

[30] Saliha B Selman and Janean E Dilworth-Bart, 'Routines and child development: a systematic review', *Journal of Family*

6. Reclaiming Freedom

not just a kid thing. Adults with regular routines and schedules are statistically less stressed, better rested, healthier and happier.[31] Therefore, it's probably neither an accident nor a coincidence that religious people – on average – tend to be happier, more fulfilled and more connected with their fellow citizens.[32] Traditional religion offers constraints in ways that appeal to the human need for meaning, inclusion, community and regularity. As the Christian thinker GK Chesterton puts it, 'orthodoxy [is] the only logical guardian of liberty, innovation and advance.'[33]

Freedom, ultimately, is not about being able to do what you want, but about doing what you can with what you've got. Good constraints embody purpose. They build meaning. They strengthen relationships. They take us out of ourselves. And at least some of them can be reduced to simple principles that we can translate into lifehacks to

---

Theory and Review, June 2024, 16(2).

[31] *Health benefits of having a routine,* Northwestern Medicine website, December 2022, accessed 12 November 2024. https://www.nm.org/healthbeat/healthy-tips/health-benefits-of-having-a-routine

[32] Shadi Hamid, 'Secular stagnation: how religion endures in a godless age,' *Foreign Affairs*, 18 June 2024, accessed 25 September 2024. https://www.foreignaffairs.com/reviews/secular-stagnation-hamid-divine-economy

[33] GK Chesterton, *The collected works of G.K. Chesterton*, vol. 1: *Heretics, Orthodoxy, The Blatchford Controversies*, Ignatius Press, San Francisco, 1986, p 346.

help us think about, share and inform our freedom in ways that build 'shalom', enhance happiness and boost wellbeing. In the words of Washington Post columnist Shadi Hamid, 'Humans are meaning-makers who seek, and are products of, an enchanted world.'[34] Community, purpose and happiness should not play second fiddle to freedom and choice. Rather, they should be served by the freedoms we protect and the choices we make. Dodging freedom's traps seems to be about doing small, simple things in everyday life that posture us beyond the endless daily sources of hustle, hurry and expectation we all live with.

i. Slowing down and paying attention

Research shows that while the internet has accelerated the trend, it isn't the main reason that human attention spans have been shrinking over the last few hundred years. The main reason – as I've already outlined – is that we're simply taking in more and more information very quickly. Everything about our freedom-driven world is moving faster. On average, we even walk[35] and

---
[34] Hamid, *Secular Stagnation*.
[35] Robert Colville, *The great acceleration: how the world is getting*

talk[36] 10% faster than we did just a few decades ago. In a fittingly ironic example of this in my own life, I recently listened to an audiobook on slowing down and making more time for rest at double speed! I hadn't even recognised the irony until I was suitably met with laughter by some friends when I casually mentioned it.

The more we take in – streaming, binge-watching, doom-scrolling and online posting – the less time and capacity we have for resting, reflecting and thinking. More speed means less comprehension. And as we whizz through life, experiencing more and more while understanding less and less, the trappings of freedom get a firmer grip on us. There are always forces and structures at work that are designed to direct and manipulate our freedom. Aspects of our modern consumer-driven economies are designed not to optimise our freedom but to direct and manipulate it. The less we pay attention, the less we think about what we're taking in. We think less about the models of success that are infused into advertising. We're less likely to moderate our use of technology. We impair our ability to properly examine the consequences

faster and faster, Bloomsbury, London, 2016, pp 1–3.

[36] Colleen Ross, 'How technology is turning us into faster talkers,' CBC News website, 31 October 2011, accessed 12 November 2024. https://www.cbc.ca/news/canada/how-technology-is-turning-us-into-faster-talkers-1.1111667

of our choices. And the less thoughtful we are in how we spend our freedom.

Author Andy Crouch suggests turning off our devices for one hour per day, one day per week and one week per year.[37] Avoiding screentime for at least one hour before bedtime improves sleep. Taking some time each day to be in silence – even for a minute or two – helps counter the continuing stream of input we're exposed to. This could take the form of meditation, prayer or simply sitting quietly. Setting aside time in your diary for rest and reflection ensures that unforeseen invitations won't swamp your schedule. Walking has been proven to reduce stress and boost cognitive function. And placing a few things on your morning wake-up routine before you pick up your phone – maybe a conversation with a loved one, a deep breath, a prayer, a glance out the window, or a cup of tea or coffee – will give your phone an overdue demotion in your hierarchy of morning priorities.

Slowing down and thinking a little more about what goes into our eyes and ears helps enable an enjoyment of freedom with greater understanding and, therefore, wiser choices. When we ration screen time, actively resist and ignore online

---

[37] Andy Crouch, *The tech-wise family: everyday steps for putting technology in its proper place*, Baker Books, Grand Rapids, 2017, p 83.

advertising suggestions, and set aside time in our diaries for resting, thinking, working, walking and physically being with other people, we increase the likelihood that we'll spend our freedom wisely. Living slower and more thoughtful lives enables us to pay better attention to our choices, their consequences and navigate the unseen forces that drive our modern consumer lifestyles. As we slow down and pay more attention, we see both the contexts and the consequences of our choices more clearly. We see that when new things are possible, there are often old things that are no longer possible. When new experiences and opportunities present themselves, they always come with implications and impacts – both for us and for those around us. Slowing down helps us navigate all of this.

ii. Limiting choice where we can

From choosing jam to pasta sauce to what we wear, a crippling array of choices is a central part of the freedom trap. Reducing our choices might seem counter-intuitive, but when done right, it can bring some badly needed simplicity to the complexity of modern life. Why not use some of our choices to, well, reduce our choices? There's plenty of conventional wisdom out there about keeping your options open. But perhaps that isn't always a good idea.

The cartoonist Allen Saunders is said to have remarked, 'Life is what happens to us while we are making other plans.'[38] It speaks to the time and effort we commit every day to making relatively unimportant choices. Meanwhile, time passes, leaving us regularly wondering why it seems like every week, month and year is disappearing more quickly than the last. Limiting our choices to what matters most frees up headspace, heart-space and time. Of course, limiting choice calls for wisdom and will look different for each of us. Furthermore, some choices *are* of particular significance and justify deep and slow consideration of options and consequences. Choosing a life partner, a place to live or a career are obvious examples. However, not all choices are equal. Both the research and common sense suggest that painstakingly pouring over colours for new curtains, outfits for the day, restaurant menu items for fear of food envy or endlessly scouring Facebook Marketplace for that 'perfect' second-hand bargain isn't the best use of our choice-making capacity. When it comes to jam, pasta sauce and the like, just think, choose

---

[38] Fred R Shapiro (ed), *The New Yale Book of Quotations*, Yale University Press, New Haven, 2021, p 716.

and get on with your life. The time and energy we spend on our decisions should be – in some way – proportionate to the significance and ongoing impact of those decisions.

At ground level, there are simple things we can do to minimise 'choice anxiety.' This isn't a book about decluttering, but it's hard to ignore the reality that owning fewer things often helps with reducing the stress of choice. Fewer jackets, shoes and hats make getting ready easier.[39] If wardrobe variety is important to you, consider sectioning off parts of your wardrobe periodically, only choosing from particular shelves and drawers for a given week or month. Locking in a pre-determined breakfast option every day – at least for a period of time before switching to another – takes the hassle out of morning food selection. And for those responsible for providing dinner for a household, keeping dinner items locked in on set days of the week works a treat. Trust me, there's nothing like counting down to fried chicken Fridays!

---

[39] The idea of a 'capsule wardrobe' dates back to the 1970s and seeks to maximise the number of possible outfits using a relatively small number of interchangeable essential items of clothing.

iii. Being kind

As we've already explored, much of the freedom trap rests on the message that you are the most important person in the world and that freedom is all about getting what you want. At the risk of sounding simplistic and idealistic, 'kindness' offers a helpful vaccination against this idea. In doing so, it helps us set up habits, mindsets and heart postures that cut against the grain of autonomy. When we look beyond ourselves and invest in relationships, we naturally live in a way that puts the interests of others first.

Admittedly, kindness is much more easily talked about and written about than practised. Inside each of us, the impulse for self-interested self-gratification always lingers. But it's not unbeatable. In the 1990s, a research team in Italy noticed that monkeys who saw a person grab a peanut experienced the same brain activity as when they grabbed one themselves. The study marked the discovery of 'mirror neurons' – cell systems in our brains that fire when we encounter someone else experiencing something. This discovery underpinned our modern understanding of empathy, which means to 'feel with' or 'suffer with'. Or, as the Bible puts it, to 'carry each other's burdens.'[40] In his book *The Master and His Emissary*, psychiatrist and neuroscientist Ian McGilchrist contends that modern society exists not because of our inventions, industry or markets but because of 'inter-subjectivity' – that is, our capacity to empathise.[41] It's not just freedom and technology that got us here, but empathy and kindness.

Building empathy is a team sport for families, neighbourhoods and nations alike. But there are small things that we can do as individuals to help the project along. Here's one you won't have to wait long to practise – wait for the next time someone does something you really dislike: cuts you off in traffic, is inexplicably rude, expresses an offensive opinion, takes your seat on the train, etc. Instead of condemning them to the seventh circle of hell in your mind, take a breath and consider what might have led them to do that. A difficult morning, a lost job, or an unrelated invisible medical or emotional struggle? Thought experiments like this aren't perfect, but they exercise our empathy pathways and remind us that most people, most of the time, are navigating difficult struggles.

---

[40] Galatians 6:2.

[41] Ian McGilchrist, *The master and his emissary: the divided brain and the making of the Western world*, Yale University Press, New Haven, 2019, pp 143–177.

The next time you come across a comment from a morally self-righteous grandstander on social media (again, sadly, this is likely to be sooner rather than later), before rushing to counterpunch with a flurry of keyboard high kicks, take a moment to ask yourself three questions:

i. Is what I'm about to say true?
ii. Is it kind?
iii. Is it necessary?

There's always plenty that could be said, but I've found that using this three-pronged filter almost always avoids wasted time, eliminates unneeded stress and saves precious headspace. Helpfully, this 'rule of three' tends to work in office meetings, family gatherings, dinner parties and, perhaps most effectively, when opportunities present themselves to offer a view about people for whom we may have a less than favourable opinion.

A commitment to kindness locates us outside of ourselves. It reminds us that regardless of our differences, we're in this together. Kindness fights *anomie* – that deterioration of shared trust and values between people. Kindness better informs how we exercise our freedom and gets us thinking more often about how our choices affect others. If healthy freedom is about finding the right limits, there probably isn't a better constraint than kindness.

iv. Investing in relationships

If kindness is the healthiest constraint to true freedom, then friendships and relationships are freedom's best objective. *New York Times* columnist Thomas Friedman observed, 'People have bodies and souls, and when you feed one and not the other you always get into trouble.'[42] Regardless of one's religious beliefs, the science invariably points to the importance of human-to-human connection as essential to our physical, mental and emotional health.

We need thicker, healthier communities that resist *anomie*. We need more shared moments, spaces, experiences and connections. The era of the individual needs to be complemented by the era of the individual in community. Social psychologist Jonathan Haidt observes that when our social order weakens, it doesn't liberate us. Instead, it leaves us lost and anxious.[43] The key to tackling modern anxiety, then, is to use some of our freedom to invest in one another.

A good way to start might be to consider how our decisions might affect our relationships. A

---
[42] Thomas Friedman, *Thank you for being late: an optimist's guide to thriving in the age of accelerations*, Picador USA, New York, 2017, p 155.
[43] Haidt, *The anxious generation*, p 194.

promotion at work, a more demanding job, a bigger home or a lucrative new side hustle might come with the promise of wealth and status. However, adding a relational dimension to our decision-making will help ensure that our connections to friends and family aren't sacrificed in the pursuit of material prosperity and conventional markers of success.

At a simpler level, adding social considerations to decision-making can help ensure that we use our freedom as relationally as possible in everyday life. For presents, we can gift experiences that can be shared: theatre tickets, restaurant vouchers, a weekend away or a bottle of wine to be enjoyed together. Try to have at least one meal each week – one-on-one – with a friend, colleague or family member. Schedule reminders to message a friend who you don't see regularly. Schedule at least half a day every week to spend time with your family (or those you consider family). If you haven't already, make an effort to get to know your neighbours. These are small and simple suggestions. There are countless others that may better suit you, but the basic principles are what matters. Growing closer to those around us begins with scheduling in time and consciously establishing small habits that better weave our lives in with the lives of those around us.

6. Reclaiming Freedom

If true freedom – as I've suggested – operates best when it's directed at life-giving purposes, there doesn't seem to be a better set of purposes out there than to invest in authentic friendships and relationships with other people. Relationships simultaneously restrict freedom (in a good way), guide our choices and enrich our lives. Freedom can't operate in a vacuum – at least not healthily. It needs broader purposes. And investing in connections with those around us – our family, our friends, our colleagues, our neighbours and our classmates – furthers the idea that we are part of something beyond ourselves. It acknowledges that my freedom must operate not just alongside the freedom of others but in interaction with the freedom of others.

An understanding that true freedom begins with other people is the difference between *Lord of the Flies* and *Lord of the Rings* – between chaos and community and between being self-driven and purpose-driven. It seems that we are best served by freedom that is underpinned by a matrix of conditions that point to a vision of the 'good life' in which we are connected to other people.

Conclusion

A look at the cogs inside the freedom machine has revealed a more complex equation than one in which people must simply throw off constraints. Freedom – if not thought through – comes with traps. They include the anxiety of unnecessary choice, the consequences of our decision-making, modern standards of success and conformity, and the increasingly unifying power of technology.

There are, of course, aspects of freedom that more obviously support ancient and enduring ideas of human dignity – the freedoms of speech, thought, assembly, religion and conscience, to name a few. However, freedom's long march through consumer culture, digital revolutions and our modern psyche has been left largely unchecked, and therefore, its trappings are often left unexamined. The quiet embellishment of 'freedom' into 'autonomy' has put us at risk of living faster, choice-raddled, disconnected, unexamined and ultimately less free lives.

Locating the purposes of our freedom in something outside of our desires and ourselves inoculates us against many of modern freedom's trappings. When done right, constraints can both augment true freedom and fuel wellbeing. Expanding the moorings of modern freedom beyond personal autonomy can relieve pressure, ease expectations, build meaning and strengthen connections. The right constraints can take us out of ourselves. By slowing down, paying attention, limiting choice, being kind and investing in our connections with others, wellbeing can be served through a refined understanding of freedom. True freedom. A way of approaching life that honours our longing to be free without ignoring our need for richer sources of meaning.

Re:CONSIDERING

ALSO AVAILABLE

Scan this code for more information

Are you an achievement addict?

It's hard not to be one given our collective obsession with success.

Students fear that the ATAR will sum up not just their schooling career, but also their individual worth. Australians aren't just mad for sporting victory – skyrocketing house prices show we're equally hooked on owning property. Then there are the furious work habits of Silicon Valley CEOs, violin prodigies, and tiger mums.

Why do we constantly strive for our significance – and could you quit the habit if you tried?

Re:CONSIDERING

ALSO AVAILABLE

Scan this code for more information

Who's in favour of compassion?

Pretty much everybody, actually.

Left or right, religious or not, nobody seems to have a bad word to say about compassion.

So why do we have so much trouble addressing the conflict, inequality, and suffering in our world?

Ranging from the streets of St Kilda to the slums of Delhi, from Plato to Nietzsche, the Dalai Lama to Peter Singer, and from *Seinfeld* to the Good Samaritan, Tim Costello appeals to our common humanity – and takes an unflinching look at how costly compassion can be.

Re:CONSIDERING

ALSO AVAILABLE

Scan this code for more information

What were you thinking?

We all feel entitled to our opinion. Whether it be our take on politics, vaccines, parenting, or the value of religion, everybody wants to have their say - and everybody loves to be right.

But do we know what it means to think well?

Covering 'idiot brain', lobotomies, the difference between certainty and confidence, the nature of facts, and the virtue of intellectual hospitality, Mark Stephens invites you to consider not just what you think but how and why you think.

Do we think only for ourselves, or also for the good of others?

Re:CONSIDERING

ALSO AVAILABLE

Scan this code for more information

Pandemic, supervolcano, late capitalism, transhumanism, populism, cancel culture, the post-antibiotic age, the gig economy, the surveillance state, the cascading effects of climate change …

Whatever the specifics, do you feel like things have gone off the rails – or are just about to?

If you've read the news, watched a zombie movie, or gotten into an argument on Twitter lately, the answer is probably yes.

And you're not alone.

What makes us such apocaholics?

What's so appealing about Armageddon? What are the pleasures – and also the perils – of our pessimism?

Re:CONSIDERING

ALSO AVAILABLE

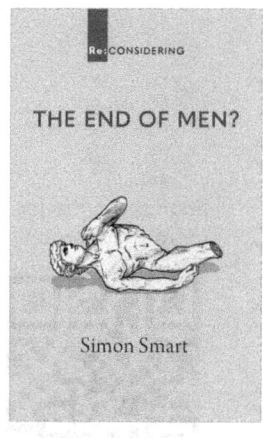

Scan this code for more information

What makes a good man?

In this grounded, forthright and hopeful book, Simon Smart reconsiders the place of boys and men in today's world.

Models of masculinity may be less constricting than they used to be – but boys and men are confused about what's expected of them, and it shows. In education, in mental health, in relationships, they're struggling. And we're all struggling to have a constructive conversation about the challenges they face.

Drawing on his own experiences of schooling and fatherhood, the best contemporary research, interviews with those on the front lines of a growing crisis, as well as ancient wisdom, Simon asks the question: how can we help boys become their best selves, and a gift to those around them?

www.ingramcontent.com/pod-product-compliance
Lightning Source LLC
Chambersburg PA
CBHW060201050426
42446CB00013B/2936